CHILDREN ADRIFT IN FOSTER CARE:

A STUDY OF ALTERNATIVE APPROACHES

Edmund A. Sherman
Renee Neuman
Ann W. Shyne

Report of a study funded by Child Welfare Research and
Demonstration Grant PR-500 from the Community Services
Administration of the United States Department of Health,
Education and Welfare.

Research Center

Child Welfare League of America, Inc.

2nd Printing 1974

$3.00
F-46

1-21-74

1805530

Acknowledgments

Because of concern in the field of child welfare about the tendency of temporary foster care to drift without plan into permanent substitute care, the CWLA Research Center staff devised strategies, suggested by the practice literature and unpublished program efforts in the field of foster care, that we thought might counteract this drift. To test the strategies, we needed an agency that not only would supply a great deal of information to us but would be willing to modify its ways of operating to incorporate the proposed interventions. The receptivity of the Rhode Island Department of Social and Rehabilitative Services to being the site for the project was highly gratifying and encouraging to the CWLA research staff.

The two persons whose support was indispensable were Anthony E. Ricci, Assistant Director, Family and Children's Services, and Catherine M. Cooney, Chief Child Care Supervisor. Mr. Ricci's enthusiasm from the start and his ready availability to resolve snags were a tremendous help, as were Miss Cooney's advice and continuous facilitating activity throughout the project. We express our appreciation to them, as well as to John J. Affleck, Director of the Department, who opened the doors of the agency to the project.

We hope that participation in the project was of some benefit to the agency, as we have no doubt that it caused many headaches for the administrative, supervisory, practitioner and clerical staff who were involved in its implementation.

We are appreciative to the agency for helping us locate the staff employed especially for the project and to these four persons who carried it out: Mrs. Margaret Farrell and Mrs. Carol Ann Weiss, who as "special workers" exemplified one of the intervention strategies we were testing; Mrs. Sally Edgren, the research interviewer; and Mrs. Martha Parks, who as the coordinator had the unenviable task of keeping track of what everyone was to do when and getting it done. A total of 19 supervisors and 65 caseworkers were actively involved in the project. We are grateful to all of the participants, but would like to recognize particularly the contribution of Mrs. Dorothy Goldblatt and Miss Sandra Piorier, who supervised the special workers.

The project was financed by a Child Welfare Research and Demonstration Grant initially from the Children's Bureau and subsequently from the Community Services Administration of the United States Department of Health, Education and Welfare. Children Adrift in Foster Care is the last of a series of reports conducted under that program research grant. We are grateful for the foresight of Dr. Charles Gershenson, who instituted the plan of program research grants, which permit a continuity of research impossible without continuity of funding. Dr. Abraham Levine, who has administered the grants program over the last few years, has been supportive of our work and patient about our delays in wrapping up several related projects that concluded almost simultaneously.

Within the League we are mindful of the support of colleagues in the various departments that is essential to the relevance and smoothness of our own operations.

CONTENTS

1. THE DEVELOPMENT OF THE STUDY 1

    Background of the Research 1
    The Problem of the Study 3
    Alternative Approaches to the Problem 5

2. THE STUDY DESIGN AND METHODS OF DATA COLLECTION 10

    The Study Setting 11
    Selection of Cases 13
    The Intervention Strategies 14
    Data Collection Procedures and Instruments 16
    Methodological Problems 19

3. THE CHILDREN AND THEIR FAMILIES 21

    Description of the Final Sample 22
    Cases Served by the Special Workers 36

4. HOW THE CHILDREN FARED 49

    The Intervention Strategies and Changes in
      Foster Care Status 49
    Factors Associated With the Implementation
      of Definite Plans 57
    The Children Who Returned to Their Parents 81
    The Children Who Received Alternate Care 90

5. DISCUSSION OF THE FINDINGS 96

    Consideration of Research Limitations 96
    Highlights of the Findings 98
    Implications for Practice 101

APPENDIX

    A. Monitoring Form 105
    B. Baseline Data on Study Child 107
    C. Evaluation Interview I 119

CHAPTER 1

THE DEVELOPMENT OF THE STUDY

Background of the Research

This demonstration developed as somewhat of a natural extension of a series of
studies conducted by the Research Center of the Child Welfare League of America.
Since 1964 the League has had a Child Welfare Research and Demonstration Grant
for a Coordinated Program of Research in Foster Care. The early studies conducted under the grant dealt primarily with foster care as a substitute service.
Some of these and earlier studies indicated that there might not have been need
to place substantial numbers of children in foster care if there had been preventive services available to the children in their own homes and if there had
been more systematic and adequate determination of the need for placement in
the first place.

With this background the Research Center turned its attention in 1969 to two
related research questions. One asked which children from what kinds of families
and situations tend to be placed in foster care and, conversely, which children
tend to be served in their own homes. If we could identify the factors that go
into the decision to place or to serve in own home, we might be able to develop
guides for more systematic and appropriate decisions by practitioners. The
second question asked what the actual content of service in own homes tended to
be, and what outcomes are associated with what types of service. Since there
were indications from prior research and practice that supportive services might

prevent the need for placement, a study of such services provided by child welfare agencies with successful outcomes might lead to a further development and extension of these services to prevent unnecessary placements.

Research addressed to these questions was conducted in four child welfare agencies. A report on the research concerning the decision to place children or serve them in their own homes was published in the latter part of 1971.[1] Then, the own-home service cases from that study were followed up for a year to determine the nature and the outcome of the service. The report on this second study was published early in 1973.[2]

While these related projects were still in progress, we were encouraged by the Children's Bureau to consider possible demonstration projects in the general area of child welfare services. It was too early to develop definitive ideas for demonstrations from either of the two ongoing projects, but after discussions with field consultants and other colleagues in the League and meetings with other researchers, we decided to undertake research into ways of returning children from foster care to their families, or in other ways to prevent the pervasive drift of temporary foster care into indefinite long-term foster care.

Since we had concerned ourselves with the question of what goes into making sound decisions about placement, and to learning the ingredients of successful service to prevent placement, it seemed a natural extension of interest in alternatives to placement to study ways of getting children out of the limbo of indefinite temporary foster care.

---

1. Michael H. Phillips et al., Factors Associated with Placement Decisions in Child Welfare (New York: Child Welfare League of America, 1971). The report of an extension of this study appeared as Phillips et al., A Model for Intake Decisions in Child Welfare (New York: Child Welfare League of America, 1972).

2. Edmund A. Sherman et al., Service to Children In Their Own Homes: Its Nature and Outcome (New York: Child Welfare League of America, 1973).

The Problem of the Study

The problem of children adrift in foster care has been a matter of recurrent concern in the child welfare field. It is a problem found in just about any area, and it is found among some of the most progressive and concerned agencies. In fact, it is usually the agencies concerned enough to study the problem that turn up facts about its actual dimensions. A recent report from a statewide agency in New Hampshire illustrates this:

> "In a Child and Family Service study of all the foster children (316) for whom four New Hampshire counties were liable in 1971: 90 had been in placement 2 to 6 years; 138 over 6 years. Of all these children, only 21 were returned home and eight adopted in that calendar year. This illustrates that the foster child is caught in a situation usually beyond his control where agencies and institutions make decisions for him and about him, and can become 'lost' in the system."[3]

Perhaps more dramatically than any other single study, Maas and Engler's Children in Need of Parents demonstrated how allowing children to drift in an indefinite state of temporary foster care tends to lock the children into the foster care system ever more firmly with the passage of time.[4] Their findings indicated that if the children were allowed to drift in this state of limbo for $1\frac{1}{2}$ or 2 years, their chances of ever leaving it were slim. The dire consequences for the child caught in this system have been well expressed by Bryce and Ehlert in their report of a study of children in foster care:

> "It is our conviction that no child can grow emotionally while in limbo, never really belonging to anyone except on a temporary and ill-defined or partial basis. He cannot invest except in a minimal way (just enough to survive) if tomorrow the relationship may be severed. To remain superficially involved can be an advantage in the temporary foster care arrangement, but it is disastrous on a long-term basis. To grow, the child needs at least the promise of permanency in relationships and some continuity of environment. Foster parents face a problem too, when they are left to rear

3. Child and Family Services of New Hampshire, Reaching Out as Family Advocates. Third Summary Report of the Family Advocacy Program (Manchester, New Hampshire: Child and Family Services of New Hampshire, 1972), pp. 11-12.

4. Henry S. Maas and Richard E. Engler, Children in Need of Parents (New York: Columbia University Press, 1959).

children who do not belong to them, especially when there is only rare contact with the agency. The foster parents cannot summon up the conviction to convey to the child convincingly that he belongs to them, that they expect certain things of him, and at times demand things of him. Even if such intensity were possible, it would mislead the child, in view of his ever-impending departure.

"In the absence of a final sense of belonging and investment, effectiveness of authority inherent in the parent-child relationship is missing. Depth, and therefore meaning, in relationship is dramatically reduced. Familial identification is not possible. It is this conviction in relationship, the defined and enduring quality of the happy and unhappy shared experiences through time, that gives meaning to and makes for durability in the relationship. If we do not provide this as the child's younger years go by, we deny the child the experience he needs to grow."[5]

Having identified this drift as a pervasive problem is of course not enough. Its existence raises the question of how it tends to come about. To speak of a child's getting "lost" in the system suggests somehow that the child has been overlooked or forgotten. It is this interpretation that leads to the frequent call for tracking systems in children's agencies.

Another explanation of the problem points to the very nature of the foster care system itself. This argument runs to the effect that when the child is placed in foster care, a transaction has taken place that tends to take the initiative and responsibility away from the natural parent, even in cases of voluntary placement, and lodge it with the agency and most particularly in the worker-foster home network. A study by Gottesfeld demonstrated that the natural parent becomes very much an outsider to this network, and that, however inadvertently, the agency/worker service focus and efforts are directed toward the child in the context of the foster home.[6] The feelings of a mother whose children were placed

---

5. Marvin E. Bryce and Roger C. Ehlert, "144 Foster Children," Child Welfare, L (November 1971), p. 503.

6. Harry Gottesfeld, "In Loco Parentis: A Study of Perceived Role Values in Foster Home Care" (New York: Jewish Child Care Association, 1970).

and who went through the "outsider" experience have been eloquently portrayed by Phyllis Johnson McAdams.[7] She indicates that a sense of failure, guilt and doubt can be debilitating for a parent and can discourage serious intentions of reestablishing a home and getting her children back. For this reason, she believes that the social workers should push visiting on the part of reluctant parents. Yet, the focus and time limitations of the workers are such that efforts tend to be geared away from the natural parent and toward the foster home, because that is where the child is. Apropos of this, another study on foster care in a large statewide public agency showed that the pattern of worker contacts was such that the foster parents were visited most frequently, the foster children second, and the natural parents a distant third.[8] This is, of course, a finding that would be repeated in agency after agency if they were to replicate such studies.

Given this background on the nature of the problem of drift in foster care, we attempted to develop and test alternative approaches to the problem.

Alternative Approaches to the Problem

A number of attempts have been made to cope with the problem of this study. One, in fact, was undertaken in an agency that was studied by Maas and Engler in their Child Welfare League Project, and the agency was found to have particularly large numbers of children adrift in its foster care system. On the basis of the negative findings of the Maas-Engler study, the agency undertook a multifaceted "shotgun" approach to the problem, including: more aggressive court action with parents who abandoned their children or who were not rehabilitatable, to free the children for adoption; giving foster parents who expressed interest in adopting

---

7. Phyllis Johnson McAdams, "The Parent in the Shadows," Child Welfare, LI (January 1972), pp. 51-55.

8. Illinois Department of Children and Family Services, A Study of Children in Foster Care 15 Months or More: Foster Care I (Springfield, Illinois: Illinois Department of Children and Family Services, October 15, 1971), p. 3.

children accelerated services to bring adoption about; intensifying case contacts with parents with a view to return home or adoption; dropping or de-emphasizing the matching of adoptive children with adoptive parents on physical, social, racial and religious grounds; and finding families who were willing to risk accepting children though there were legal obstacles to adoption to overcome.[9] On the basis of these efforts, the agency reported: "In the second year after the League study, the adoptive rate was more than doubled. Nearly doubled also was the turnover rate of children leaving foster care to go home."[10]

In developing strategies for a demonstration project, we focused on what appeared to be two separate but related elements in the problem as it has been outlined in the foregoing section. The first element had to do with the children getting "lost" in the system, which meant doing something about keeping track of them. The second element had to do with the natural parents getting "lost" or locked out of the foster care network of worker-child-foster home, which appeared to be related to the first element, since many children got lost because their parents were lost in terms of rehabilitation or planning.

Proposals for dealing with the first element of the problem have been around for a long time. Over 20 years ago Mary Lewis advocated the development of casework plans for each child in foster care, to be reviewed at regular intervals, and monthly statistical reporting on the status of children in care.[11] The very nature of the problem immediately suggests this type of approach. We therefore determined that one of the intervention strategies we would test would be a

---

9. Joseph Paull, "An Agency Cleans House," Child Welfare, XXXIX (January 1960), pp. 19-21.

10. Ibid., p. 21.

11. Mary Lewis, "Long-Time Temporary Placement," Child Welfare, XXX (January 1951), pp. 3-7.

monitoring system in which the workers would be held accountable for the current status of the children, would have to develop plans for more permanent care, and would have to report periodically on their efforts to implement those plans.

The second element of the problem is only partly addressed by the monitoring strategy. Although the foster care workers would be held accountable in a monitoring system for contacts with natural parents in order to engage in planning for more permanent arrangements, we were aware that such a reporting system might not have the impact or urgency about it to affect significantly the frequency of contact with natural parents. It is, after all, common for forms designed to systematize a process to become "routine" and to lose their urgency for the persons responsible for filling them out.

One strategy that suggested itself for dealing with the problem of loss of contact with the natural parents was the use of special workers whose primary responsibility would be to work intensively with the natural parents. This approach was being tried out by a member agency of the Child Welfare League at the time this study was being planned.[12] The main features and criteria of the program were: The families selected for the project had to be recently known to the agency; the service given to them would be intensive and time-limited (clients seen on a weekly basis for 6 months); one or both natural parents had to be available for contact with the worker; the regular foster care workers would continue to provide service to the children and their foster families; and the special worker would continue supervision of the child in the natural parent home after discharge from foster care.

---

12. Baltimore County Department of Social Services, Pilot Project: Experience with a Specialized Caseload of Natural Parents (Towson, Maryland: Baltimore County Department of Social Services, 1971), Mimeographed.

Most of the features of this program looked as though they could be implemented in most agency settings. The numbers involved in the project were small, however, with one worker handling 11 families in the 6-month period--too small a number to show statistically significant impact. There have probably been similar projects in other agencies, but to our knowledge there have been none that were set up with a predesigned and systematic evaluative research scheme.

The project just described was geared toward return of the children to their natural parents. Although we intended this to be a major objective of our demonstration, we were aware that return to the parents might not be possible or advisable for some children in indefinite temporary foster care. Adoption would, of course, be one way out for some of these children, and that seemed to be the primary focus of the agency that "cleaned house," as described by Paull (footnote 9). Where adoption is not possible, though, because of the age of the child or the attitude of the natural parents, some other scheme to give the child a sense of permanency becomes necessary.

Madison and Shapiro have indicated that ". . . agencies are finding oral or written contracts useful in creating a feeling of permanence and security and easing the child's search for identity."[13] Weinstein's research on the self-image of the foster child tends to support this interpretation of the value of planned permanent foster care.[14] We anticipated, therefore, that some kind of contractual permanent or long-term foster care would have to be one of the options in any demonstration designed to counteract the drift in foster care. This option would also obviously call for more intensive work with the natural parents to make an impact on the problem.

---

13. Bernice Madison and Michael Shapiro, "Permanent and Long-Term Foster Family Care as a Planned Service," Child Welfare, IL (March 1970), p. 136.

14. Eugene Weinstein, The Self-Image of the Foster Child (New York: Russell Sage Foundation, 1960).

It can be seen from the foregoing review that the strategies we chose to test in this demonstration were not new or innovative. The only thing new about the demonstration was the effort to build in an evaluation scheme for assessing the effectiveness of these strategies in a systematic way.

We were not necessarily sanguine about the outcome of the strategies from a statistical point of view. We knew from prior research by Fanshel, Jenkins, Murphy and others (cited and discussed in Chapter 4) that there were powerful antecedent variables, such as age of the child and length of time already spent in foster care, that would be difficult for any experimental program variables (strategies) to overcome. Even if these antecedent variables were evenly distributed among the children in the experimental and control groups, it would take considerable time and numbers of children to show statistically significant results. As it turned out, we did not have the time and numbers we would have liked. Our original proposal was geared toward testing in two large agencies with heavy foster care loads for a minimal period of 16 months. We had to settle for one agency and a 12-month period, because of budgetary limitations. However, the importance of the problem of children in limbo in foster care impelled us to undertake this demonstration. It was not just a question of whether these specific strategies "work" or not. It was also important to know how they do or do not work. Finally, there was much to learn in systematically studying the process and the constraints involved in extricating the children from this limbo.

CHAPTER 2

THE STUDY DESIGN AND METHODS OF DATA COLLECTION

To test the effectiveness of the intervention strategies suggested to counteract
the drift in foster care--an administrative control device and the assignment of
special caseworkers to work with natural families--we proposed a field demonstration in two operating agencies. In each agency we planned to divide the foster
care staff into three segments, to introduce the experimental programs in two of
these and to utilize the third segment, which would have no new input, as a
control or basis of comparison with the two experimental programs. As noted,
limitations in funding necessitated confining the demonstration to a single
agency, a feasible plan because the design called for comparison within each
agency. A second agency would have provided a concurrent replication, but it
was not essential to implementation of the design.

Our first tasks were to locate an appropriate agency setting, to define the range
of cases to be included, to design the intervention strategies, and to develop
procedures for collecting the data needed in circumscribing the study population,
allocating cases to the three segments of the program, and evaluating their
relative effectiveness.

The Study Setting

A first essential was to locate a child care agency appropriate as a setting for the demonstration. What makes an agency appropriate? Since the problem of drift in foster care was believed most likely to arise in large public agencies, our first criterion was that the setting be a public child welfare agency with a substantial number of children in foster care. If an agency was to involve itself in the disruption inevitably caused by a research demonstration, it had to be concerned about the research problem. Also, the agency had to have specialized foster care caseloads organized in units, so that these units could be combined to form the two experimental segments and the control segment.

In the fall of 1970 we wrote to several public agencies affiliated with the Child Welfare League, describing the general plan of the project and inquiring into their concern with the problem, the organization of their caseloads, and their interest in participation. Most, but not all, of the agencies were concerned with the problem. Most, but not all, had specialized foster care caseloads. Some of the agencies that met these criteria could not, for various reasons, accommodate the demonstration. Our final selection was the Child Welfare Services (later called simply Child Welfare) of the Rhode Island Department of Social and Rehabilitative Services. The agency seemed well suited in size and organization of caseloads, and both the Department Director and the Administrator of Child Welfare Services were enthusiastic about the agency's participation and lent strong support to implementation of the demonstration. Its location within easy travel of New York was a great asset, since monthly visits by the study director proved to be important to smooth operations.

As described in the last annual report of the Department of Social and Rehabilitative Services, "specialized child welfare functions carried by the Child Welfare unit within Family and Children's Services are designed to prevent family breakdown, to provide protection to children in danger of being neglected or abused, and to provide placement for children who must live away from their own families or need separation from their families for some hours during the day as a treatment plan for the child and the family."[1] In addition to responsibility for social studies of children of concern to the Family Court and for licensing and maintenance of standards for care of children away from their families, the Child Welfare unit provides the following preventive and rehabilitative social services:

1. Services to children and their families in their own homes.

2. Protective services to neglected and abused children and their parents.

3. Foster care--in foster homes and group settings.

4. Shelter care for children temporarily without a caretaker.

5. Day care in family day care homes.

6. Adoption placement for children under the care of the agency.

7. Service to unmarried mothers for whom the agency has a prior responsibility.

On June 30, 1970, the close of the fiscal year preceding the project, the unit was serving 4809 children, with the majority receiving service in their own homes. Child Welfare Services had a total staff of 202, including 111 social caseworkers and 33 administrative and supervisory personnel. In December 1970, when the demonstration was being planned, Child Welfare Services had 920 children in foster care, exclusive of 209 children being supervised in the homes of relatives. Service to these children was being provided by 37 caseworkers in 10

---

1. Department of Social and Rehabilitative Services, Division of Community Services, Family and Children's Services, Child Welfare. Report for Year Ending June 30, 1972.

supervisory units, some of which had foster care workers only and others of which included protective and home service workers. One supervisory unit was made up of five caseworkers carrying caseloads of children in institutions, either the Department's Children's Center or private institutions with specialized programs. The Adoption Unit, which had 38 children in adoptive placement at the end of fiscal 1970, makes adoptive placements only of babies of unmarried mothers already known to the agency or children committed to the agency for whom adoption proves to be the best plan.

Considerable reorganization occurred within the Department in the course of the project, but this did not alter substantially the Child Welfare unit program or structure. The number of children being served had increased to 5454 as of June 30, 1972. A subsidized adoption program had been instituted and an amendment had been made in the law relating to adoption that was expected to facilitate termination of parental rights, but these changes were too new to have affected practice.

Selection of Cases

Since the initial focus of the demonstration was on strategies to facilitate the child's return home when desirable, it was decided to focus on the children in foster care for whom return home seemed most likely. We were concerned with those children for whom foster care had not already become permanent or quasi-permanent. Maas and Engler's findings suggest that staying in care beyond 2 years greatly increases the likelihood of the child's remaining in foster care.[2] We decided initially to focus our attention on children in care less than 2 years, but modified this to less than 3 years since the last separation from the child's natural or adoptive parents, in order to increase the number of children in the sample.

2. Maas and Engler, op. cit., pp. 350-351.

Because of the special problems in making permanent care arrangements for teenage children, we limited the study population to children under 13 years of age. Our third restriction was that the child have at least one natural parent whose parental rights had not been terminated and who was in the "community," that is, within the agency's geographical boundaries so that assigned caseworkers could maintain inperson contact with the natural family.

Within the agency selected the study group was further delimited to children in foster family homes or the Children's Center. Children in shelter care were omitted because such care was temporary by agency definition and usage. Children in adoptive homes were excluded, on the other hand, because such placements were permanent by plan. Children placed with relatives were not included because they were with their own families, if not their own parents. Finally, we excluded children in private institutions because of the administrative difficulty of applying our proposed strategies outside the agency where the demonstration was sited.

The plan therefore was to include all children in foster homes or the Children's Center as of March 1, 1971, who were under 13 years of age, had not been in care more than 3 years and who had a natural parent in the community, as well as all children meeting the criteria who were admitted to such care over the next 8 months. Intake to the project was cut off at the end of that time to allow at least 4 months of exposure to the demonstration program.

The Intervention Strategies

One intervention strategy, an administrative control or case monitoring plan, was designed to combat the danger of children getting "lost in the system." It consisted of a report form to be filled out by the caseworker on each study child every 3 months unless the child was discharged from foster care or entered "permanent" foster care before the date when the form was due.

This simple one-page form (see Appendix A) called for the worker to check his plan for the child and to note briefly what factors in child, parents and external circumstances interfered with implementing the plan, what activities the worker had carried out in the last 3 months to accomplish the plan, and what activities toward this end he planned for the next 3 months. The form was filled out in duplicate, with one copy retained by the worker and one copy going to the supervisor, who forwarded it to the research coordinator.

The form thus served as a reminder both to the worker and the supervisor of the status of every child and of activities on his behalf. The form could not be forgotten, as the research coordinator followed up on missing forms on the study cases.

The second strategy called for the addition of two caseworkers, whose role was described as follows in the Project Manual: "Their role is to supplement the activities of the regular or area worker by working with the natural (or adoptive) parents of selected children in the study group. Their objective will be to facilitate the child's return home by assisting the parents in altering whatever situation or attitudes interfere with the child's return, or to clarify the need for alternative plans if, after all reasonable effort, it is apparent that return home would not be in the best interests of the child." The regular workers were encouraged to refer cases that showed potential for return home, rather than those with little potential. On the other hand, they were discouraged from involving the special worker in situations where return home, or fulfillment of any other definite plan, was likely to occur without additional staff input. In other words, the efforts of the special workers were to be focused on cases that were neither "dead ends" nor "shoo-ins," but where their efforts might have some impact.

By plan, persons without graduate social work degrees but with experience in public child welfare were selected for the role of special worker, since we were interested in demonstrating results that might be accomplished with the type of personnel usually employed in public child welfare agencies. One had a bachelor's degree and $3\frac{1}{2}$ years of experience in the study agency. The other had one year of graduate social work training and several years of experience in the Rhode Island Department and elsewhere.

The monitoring system was applied in two of the three agency segments. It was used as the only modification of procedure or practice in the "monitoring segment." It was also introduced in the "special worker segment" to permit sorting out the impact of the addition of specialized staff over and above any effect of the monitoring system. The third segment was to operate as usual and serve as a control or basis of comparison.

Data Collection Procedures and Instruments

Procedures were needed for collecting data to identify the study population, to structure the agency segments, and to evaluate the relative effects, if any, of the two strategies that were introduced.

So that eligible children could be identified, staff were asked to complete an Identifying Data Form on all children in placement as of January 1, 1971, and those coming into placement through October 31, 1971. This one-page form covered only items of information needed in order to know if the child met the criteria for inclusion (birthdate, date of last separation from family, type of placement, legal status, and whereabouts of parents).

The forms collected prior to the start of the demonstration identified 312 children who fitted the study criteria. The supervisory units were divided into three segments, each of which included approximately 100 children. Children entering placement in the next 8 months brought the study group up to 413 children.

On each child in all three segments in the initial study group or later screened into it, a Baseline Data on Study Child Form was requested from each worker (see Appendix B). This 12-page form covered chiefly information on the child's admission to foster care, the functioning of the child and the parents at time of admission, the child's potential for return home, the worker's plan for the child, and an assessment of the child's total well-being. This information was obtained to permit identifying any factors that might differentiate children who remained in foster care from those who returned home in the course of the demonstration, or who had some alternate plan implemented.

When a child returned home, or at the end of the project year if the child was still in foster care, the worker was asked to submit a Worker Outcome Schedule. The purpose of this form was to record any changes in functioning and in worker's plans, and to determine the likelihood of the child's remaining home if he had returned there or of his returning home if still in care.

The effectiveness of the monitoring system and special worker activities was to be evaluated on two bases. One was the relative rates of return home or implementation of other definite plans in the three segments. It might be noted that it was not feasible to compare such rates for the project year with the prior year because data were not available for children of the particular age group, family status and duration of care included in the project. Compiling such comparative data would have necessitated abstracting the information from individual case records.

From the start we had some concern that the focus of the project on maximizing return home might lead staff to implement plans for return that might not be in the best interests of the child. A mere increase in numbers or rates could not be regarded as a successful outcome of the strategies introduced unless the return home was conducive to the child's welfare. To obtain an independent judgment of the desirability or success of the child's return to his family, a highly experienced and professionally trained social worker visited the home shortly after the child's return and 4 months later to interview the parents and to assess their functioning, the well-being and functioning of the child, and the probability of the child's being able to remain with his family. The research interviewer, who was free to structure these interviews as she considered appropriate, was guided by a detailed schedule calling for judgments in many of the areas on which the caseworker had reported (see Appendix C for Evaluation Interview I). The interviewer did not know in advance from which of the three agency segments the child had come. We anticipated that she would learn this in the course of the interviews from the parents' reference to the caseworkers, but this happened infrequently, as the parents tended not to refer to the workers by name.

Although the original focus of the demonstration on return home was expanded to the implementation of any definite plan to take the child out of the limbo of temporary foster care, our independent evaluation of the plans was restricted to the returns to the natural parents. Other plans--adoption, entering the home of relatives, permanent foster care, or admission to an institution for specialized care--removed the child from limbo, but their implementation might or might not be judged by an independent observer as desirable.

Methodological Problems

A general problem in conducting this demonstration was the time constraints. As the service phase was limited to 1 year, and the special workers necessarily built up their caseloads gradually, they had little time to work with some of the families. The followup period of 4 months was also shorter than would have been desirable to assess the success of the returns home that were accomplished.

One methodological problem to do with time was the period in which effects of the demonstration should logically be observed. Could the strategies introduced be thought to have had any influence on plans implemented during the first week or two of the demonstration? We thought not. How long should these new procedures be followed before one could logically regard returns home as resultants? Four months made some sense, as workers would have been asked for a second monitoring form on cases in the initial study group and the special workers would have had time to make visible service input. We were loath, however, to reduce further our modest sample size, and time constraints did not permit extension of the intake phase. We therefore compromised with 1 month, and disregarded only those cases on which plans were implemented within the first month of the demonstration.

Another type of problem, unrelated to time, was that of transfer of study cases from one segment to another. Our pragmatic solution was to treat the case as belonging to the segment where it was located for the longest time during the study period. This, of course, lessened the "purity" of the segments, and incidentally created some delay in data processing.

The purity of the segments may also have been diluted by the fact that the staffs of the three segments were housed together, so that all foster care staff were aware of the project and the commitment of the agency to combat the drift in foster care. It is our impression, however, that the influence on the results of any spillover of the demonstration into the control segment was minor as compared with factors not directly related to the project. We had selected an agency that was relatively well staffed, that had good administrative procedures, including the beginnings of a monitoring system, and that was strongly committed to prevention of placement and to reestablishing the child with his family whenever possible. Undoubtedly there was some room for improvement, which is one reason the agency administrators were interested in having us undertake the demonstration, but the agency was probably already trying to do more than many with the problem to which our intervention was addressed.

CHAPTER 3

THE CHILDREN AND THEIR FAMILIES

As noted in Chapter 2, a total of 312 children were identified as meeting the criteria of the study as of March 1, 1971, when the service demonstration part of the project began. An additional 110 children who met the study criteria were added to that initial group through new placements in foster care up to October 31, 1971, the cutoff date for intake into the project. The resulting total figure of 422 children was the basis for a preliminary analysis of the data previously reported.[1] However, one child died, and eight children who were discharged from foster care in the first month of the demonstration (March 1971) were dropped from the sample, because we did not think that the discharge of any children in the first month could be attributed to the intervention strategies. Consequently, the final size of the study sample was 413 children. The following description of the children and their families is based upon this figure.

This chapter describes first the children in the total study sample and their families. It then gives attention to the much smaller number of children with whom the special workers were concerned, and the service input these workers made.

---

1. Ann W. Shyne et al., "Filling a Gap in Child Welfare Research: Service for Children in Their Own Homes," Child Welfare, LI (November 1972), p. 571.

Description of the Final Sample

In describing the total sample, note is made of any variations in the character-istics of the children in the three study segments, since such variations could affect the outcomes for children in the different segments. Where variations among the segments appear, we anticipate the outcome data given in Chapter 4 and indicate whether or not the particular variable was found to have any rela-tion to outcome.

It was noted in Chapter 2 that the sample was initially divided into three segments of approximately equal size. The distribution of the 312 cases among the three segments when the demonstration started on March 1, 1971, was: first segment (control)--106 children, or 34%; second segment (monitoring form)--105 children, or 34%; and third segment (special worker)--101 children, or 32%.

The plan for admitting new children to the sample as they were placed in foster care was to take them just as they came in through regular agency intake. The only stipulation was that they meet the criteria for inclusion in the study sample. Since children meeting these criteria in the original group of 312 were fairly evenly distributed among the three segments, we assumed that the new children admitted by regular intake in the ensuing 8 months would be about evenly divided among the three segments. However, segments 1 and 2 (control and monitoring, respectively) had a somewhat disproportionate number of new placements added to their totals, while segment 3 retained and had transferred into it a somewhat higher proportion of children who had already been in foster care for considerable time. As noted in Chapter 2, when foster children were transferred to caseloads in different segments of the study during the project they were counted, for the purposes of analysis, in the segment in which they spent the most time. The final distribution of the 413 cases by segments was as follows:

Table 3.1

The Final Distribution of Children by Study Segments

Segments	Number	Percentage
1--Control	138	33
2--Monitoring Only	149	36
3--Special Worker	126	31
Total	413	100

Although the proportions of cases in the three segments are not much different from those in the initial group of 312, the processes of intake and transfer resulted in significant differences among segments on the important variable of length of time in foster care. This variable did have an effect on the outcome or final disposition of study cases, as is described in detail in Chapter 4. The final distribution of cases by segments and by length of current stay in foster care is illustrated in Table 3.2.

Table 3.2

Length of Current Stay in Foster Care by
Study Segments

Length of Current Stay in Foster Care (at time of admission to study)	1 Control		2 Monitoring Only		3 Special Worker		Total	
	#	%	#	%	#	%	#	%
Under 3 months	43	31	58	39	27	21	128	31
3 to 6 months	13	9	8	5	8	6	29	7
6 months to 1 year	33	24	22	15	18	14	73	18
1 to 1½ years	19	14	21	14	31	25	71	17
1½ to 2 years	10	7	13	9	18	14	41	10
2 to 2½ years	12	9	13	9	16	13	41	10
2½ to 3 years	8	6	14	10	8	6	30	7
Total	138	100	149	100*	126	100*	413	100

$X^2 = 25.41$, 12 df, $p < .02$

*Throughout this report percentage totals are shown as 100, even when a column adds to 99 or 101 because of rounding.

It can be seen that the third segment ended up with over half of its cases (58%) in foster care for 1 year and more, whereas the first segment had only 36% and the second segment had 42%. That the differences among the study segments on this variable are statistically significant will have to be taken into account. It is possible that the same processes that led to a higher proportion of children with longer time in foster care in the third segment also led to some differences in other characteristics or variables between the study segments.

Characteristics of the Children

The age distribution of the children in the sample did not, however, appear to be affected by the differences in length of time in current foster care. Despite differences in length of time in care, there were no significant differences among the segments in the children's ages. Table 3.3 gives the distribution for the total sample.

Table 3.3

Age of Study Children at Time of Current
Admission to Foster Care

Age	Number	Percentage
Under 1 year	76	18
1 to 3 years	103	25
3 to 5 years	74	18
5 to 7 years	56	14
7 to 9 years	47	11
9 to 11 years	37	9
11 to 13 years	20	5
Total	413	100

Well over half of the children in the sample (61%) were under 5 years of age at the time of their admission to their current foster care placement, with the modal age interval at 1 to 3 years (25%).

By far the majority of the children were in foster family care (347, or 84%) rather than in group care in the Children's Center (66 children, or 16% of the sample). There were no differences among the segments in terms of type of facility, with the children in Children's Center, by design, very evenly divided among the segments: 21 (15%) in the first segment, 24 (16%) in the second segment, and 21 (17%) in the third segment.

Another variable on which there were no differences between the study segments was sex of the child. In all, there were 226 boys, making up 55% of the sample, as compared with 187 girls, or 45%.

The ethnicity or race of the children in the sample is given in Table 3.4.

Table 3.4

Race of Study Children

Child's Race	Number	Percent
White	308	75
Black	72	17
Mixed Black/White	17	4
*Other	11	3
Unknown or No Information	5	1
Total	413	100

*Other includes: Filipino, Filipino/White, American Indian/White, and Puerto Rican.

The study segments differed significantly on the variable of race, with the second segment (monitoring only) having considerably more black children than the other two segments. This is explained by the fact that one of the supervisory units in the second segment covered an inner-city area of Providence with a predominantly black population. Since we did not break up supervisory units (except for the one unit of Children's Center cases) in constructing the study segments, this particular unit made its impact felt on the racial distribution of children in the second segment. However, it may be well to note that the race of the child showed no statistically significant relationship to the outcome variable of the study--i.e., implementation of a definite plan. In other words, there were not significantly more nor less nonwhite children who were returned to their parents, placed in adoptive homes, in special placement, or in permanent foster care, or discharged to relatives.

One variable that did have bearing on outcome, however, was the reason for the child's current foster care placement, but on this there were no substantial differences among the segments. Table 3.5 gives the breakdown of reasons that apply to the sample.

Table 3.5

Reason for Current Placement in Foster Care

Reason for Placement	Number	Percentage
Parent's Emotional Problems or Mental Illness	133	32
Neglect or Abuse of Child	86	21
Parent Unwilling to Care for Child	70	17
Family Problem	36	9
Antisocial Behavior of Parent	22	5
Environmental Problems (financial need or inadequate housing)	20	5
Child's Emotional or Behavioral Problem	18	4
Parent's Physical Illness or Disability	15	4
Other (physical handicap or mental retardation of child; death or employment of care-taking parent)	13	3
Total	413	100

Of immediate interest is the predominance of parents' emotional problems or mental illness as the reason for placement of the child. Since this category excluded the antisocial behavior of the parents (noted separately on the list of reasons), it is all the more impressive, accounting for almost one-third (32%) of the admissions. Neglect, running a rather distant second with 21%, and parents' unwillingness to care for the child, with 17%, stand considerably higher in frequency than any of the other reasons for placement.

The very small number of admissions (18, or just under 4%) attributed to the emotional or behavior problem of the child is in dramatic contrast to the predominance of the parents' emotional or behavioral problems. This finding, beyond the realistic expectation that the parents' problems will be visited upon their children, is probably explained in part by a general reluctance among child welfare workers to attribute the main or precipitating source of a problem to the child. An example of this was a case in the sample in which the worker described the problem on the Baseline Data Form as follows: "Child caused physical damage to a younger sibling; playing with matches and threatening to burn the house and destroy his mother." Yet, this worker checked off "Parent/child conflict" (included in "Family Problem" in Table 3.5) rather than "Child's Emotional or Behavioral Problem" as the main reason for placement.

Apropos of the children's emotional and behavioral adjustment, we were interested in knowing how this sample of foster care children would score on Weinstein's scale of Child's Total Well-Being, which he applied to the sample of foster children in his study, The Self-Image of the Foster Child.[2] The children were scored by their foster care caseworkers in this study on the Baseline Data Form (see Appendix B). The question underlying the scale is: To what extent does this child have the physical, intellectual, emotional and social abilities and

---

2. Weinstein, op. cit., p. 65.

resources to weather his life situations? The score is a total, global assessment of a child's well-being. The definitions of each scale position can be read in their entirety in the Baseline Data Form. Table 3.6 gives the distribution of the children in this sample as rated by the caseworkers.

Table 3.6

Distribution of Study Children on Scale of Total Well-Being

Child's Total Well-Being	Number	Percentage
Extremely high	2	< 0.5
Markedly high	35	8
Slightly above average	52	13
About average	138	33
Slightly below average	79	19
Markedly low	56	14
Extremely low	14	3
Unknown or not answered	6	1
Scale not applicable--child too young	31	8
Total	413	100

The modal scale position for this group of children is clearly "about average."
There is a moderate but distinct tendency toward more children in the lower scale positions than in the higher ones. Weinstein used a scoring system for the seven scale positions going from 0 for "extremely low" to 6 for "extremely high," with the "about average" position having a score of 3. The sample children showed a mean score of 2.73, somewhat under the midpoint or average score of 3.

It is of interest to note how this sample compares with the children in Weinstein's study. He found that the group of children who scored highest were those who clearly identified their natural parents as their "parents."[3] Those 17 children had a mean score of 3.29. The next highest group in total well-being were 28 children who identified their foster parents as their "parents," and they scored a mean of 2.50. The group scoring lowest were 16 children who were very "mixed" and unclear as to whether they should consider their natural or foster parents as their parents. They had a mean score of 2.19. The present study sample scored higher than the "foster" and "mixed" identification groups, but lower than the group identifying their natural parents. It is likely that the foster children in this sample represent a mix of the three types of parental identification. If anything, the comparison is somewhat favorable for this study sample, as the average score for Weinstein's sample when the three groups are combined is 2.66, a little lower than our 2.73.

Family Circumstances

Turning now to the family circumstances of the children in this study, Table 3.7 shows the composition of the household from which the child entered his current placement in foster care.

The most frequent type of household from which the study children were placed was clearly that headed by the mother only. So-called "intact" families (both parents in the household) were much in the minority in this sample. Only 98, or 24%, of the children came from intact families. A total of 302 children were admitted to foster care from a household that included a mother and 144 from a household that included a father.

---

3. Ibid., p. 68

Table 3.7

Household From Which Child Was Last Admitted To Foster Care

Adults in Household	Number	Percentage
Mother only	140	34
Both parents	92	22
Both parents and other adults	6	1
Father only	40	10
Mother and other adults	64	16
Father and other adults	6	1
Other adults only	38	9
No adults (e.g., abandonment, parents deceased)	18	4
No answer	9	2
Total	413	100

Table 3.8 indicates the number of other children from the family admitted to foster care at the same time as the study child.

Table 3.8

Other Children Admitted to Foster Care at the Same Time

Other Children	Number	Percentage
None	169	41
One	90	22
Two	67	16
Three	39	9
Four	26	6
Five or more	20	5
No answer	2	< 0.5
Total	413	100

Although the single most frequent situation was the placement of the study child and none other (41%), this accounted for considerably less than half the cases. Thus, about three-fifths of the placements were multiple placements of children from the same household.

Another aspect of the family situation at the time of placement was the public assistance status. We had reason to believe, from a prior CWLA study, that this variable might prove significant in the placement/discharge picture of this foster care sample.[4] As is indicated in Chapter 4, the return of children from this sample was significantly associated with the public assistance status of the family at discharge. For the moment, however, our concern is descriptive. The families of the majority of the children (62%) were receiving full public assistance and another 19% were receiving supplementary public assistance at the time of placement. Since over four out of five of the children's families whose public assistance status was known(N=377) were receiving assistance, our data concerning the families' weekly income were not meaningful in any statistical or descriptive sense. There were only 31 cases in which earned (non-PA) income was known and of those 23, or about three out of four, were earning less than $150 a week. There was little variation among segments in the proportion of families receiving public assistance.

Among the characteristics and circumstances of the families at the start of the study is one variable of central interest because it is descriptive of the involvement of the natural families with the children in foster care. This variable is the mother's contact with the child in foster care during the period (at least a month) immediately preceding the completion of the Baseline Data Form by the caseworker. This question did not apply, of course, to a number of

---

4. Phillips et al., op. cit.

children who were placed during the study and on whom the workers made out a form soon thereafter. It did, however, apply to the vast majority of cases in the sample, and the data concerning it are presented in Table 3.9.

Table 3.9

Frequency of Mother's Contact With Child in Foster Care

Frequency of Contact	Number	Percentage
At least once a week	23	6
About once in two weeks	40	10
About once a month	93	22
Some contact, but less than once a month	82	20
No contact	110	27
Not applicable--child in care less than 1 month	57	14
Not answered or unknown	8	2
Total	413	100

It is noteworthy that the largest single group had "no contact," although the group that visited about once a month is almost as large. Perhaps the most interesting information in Table 3.9 is that only about one-sixth of the mothers visited more frequently than once a month. This is consistent with the references made in Chapter 1 to the natural mother's position in the foster care situation, and the possibility of her feeling constrained by the situation from visiting more frequently. We do not, however, have data bearing directly on that possibility, so this is speculation.

The Caseworker's Plan

A variable interesting from a comparative as well as a descriptive point of view was the worker's plan for the child. Although we recognized that any definite plan that might be implemented for a child was not necessarily, and never entirely, up to the agency worker, we thought that this item on the Baseline Data Form would give some estimate of the projected outcomes for the children in the sample. Table 3.10 gives the information concerning this sample.

Table 3.10

Worker's Plan for the Child

Plan	Number	Percentage
No plan as yet	136	33
Return to parents	131	32
Permanent foster care	113	27
Adoption	26	6
Placement with relatives	1	< 0.5
Specialized placement (e.g., residential treatment)	6	1
Total	413	100

There were some differences among the segments in the worker's plan. For whatever reason, segment 2 had fewer cases with no plan, and segment 1 had fewer children expected to return home. These figures are presented and discussed along with the worker's final plan in Chapter 4 (see Table 4.4).

The figure of immediate concern in Table 3.10 is the estimate of 32% of the children with a plan for return to parents. We had anticipated that this would be the largest single plan group, but it is not much larger than the permanent foster care group. The figure of 27% for the latter was somewhat of a surprise, because the expressed philosophy of the agency was to return children to their

-33-

parents and not to retain them in long-term foster care. The administrators and supervisory staff had expected that very few permanent foster care plans would be projected. The workers, however, faced with the task of assessing the actual caseloads, turned out to be less sanguine. If we had used the more euphemistic expression "long-term" foster care in place of "permanent," it is likely that the estimate would have been even higher.

The worker's plans for the children in this sample may be compared with the findings from other settings. We have noted in reports of some member agencies of the Child Welfare League estimates of about 20% of the children in their existing foster care caseloads expected to return to their natural parents. However, their estimates were based on the total foster care caseload, which included large proportions of children who had been in care longer than the 3-year limit set for this sample, thus lowering the likelihood of return to parents.

The 32% estimate of return in this sample is not high when compared with the estimate reported by Bryce and Ehlert from their study, referred to in Chapter 1.[5] They indicate that the recorded casework plan at the time of placement was: rehabilitation of the parents (return to parents) 57%; long-term (equivalent of "permanent" in this study) 19%; no plan 15%; adoption 5%; and "special needs" ("special placement" in this study) 4%. It should be noted, however, that their sample estimate was based on casework plans at the time of placement. If they had included cases of children in care up to 3 years, as in this study, their estimate for return home probably would have been lower, and their estimate of "long-term" foster care would also probably have been closer to the estimate for permanent foster care in this study.

---

5. Bryce and Ehlert, op. cit., p. 500.

One further descriptive variable that has a bearing on the projections was the caseworker's judgment of the length of time the child would continue in care away from the parents' home. The distribution on this item, given in Table 3.11, does not appear consistent with the data on plan for the child in Table 3.10. For one thing, the worker was asked to estimate the probable time in care away from home even if he reported "no plan." His time estimates were also influenced by his degree of certainty about being able to carry out his projected plan.

Table 3.11   **1805530**

Caseworker's Judgment of Length of Care of
Child Away From Home

Worker's Judgment	Number	Percentage
Under 3 months	20	5
3 months to 6 months	29	7
6 months to 1 year	40	10
1 year to 3 years	89	22
3 years or more, but not permanently	50	12
Permanently	155	38
Unknown, not applicable, or no answer	30	7
Total	413	100

The largest judgment category in Table 3.11--permanent care away from home--should not be considered identical to the permanent foster care category of Table 3.10. The difference in the figures for the two categories, 38% and 27%, respectively, is explained by the fact that those children who would be away from home permanently could also include, in Table 3.11, those projected for adoption or specialized placement, as well as some for whom there was no plan as yet, but for whom return home would be an impossibility.

A final point should be made about the figures in Table 3.11. A total of 22% of the sample was expected to remain away from home less than a year. This figure should be used in assessing how closely the actual number of children returned home during the project (11 months) met expectations, not the figure of 32% in Table 3.10, which includes children projected for return home beyond a year.

Cases Served by Special Workers

We knew that the very process of selection of cases for the special workers would probably lead to some differences in their caseloads. We wanted to know how their cases differed from the general sample, since this information would have implications for use elsewhere. After discussing the process of selection of the cases and any differences in their characteristics we describe the services provided by the special workers and the way in which they were provided.

Selection of Cases

At the start of the project on March 1, 1971, the two workers were assigned to and housed in two different supervisory units with heavy foster care caseloads within the same study segment (third). They worked closely with the other workers in their respective units in going over the cases to identify which ones could benefit most from extensive contact with the natural parents. They worked also with workers from other units in the same segment and with certain workers carrying cases in the Children's Center, since the Center caseload was broken up equally among the three study segments.

The plan was to have the special workers work exclusively with the natural parents, while the regular foster care workers would continue to work with the child and the foster parents. It was of course expected that the special workers would meet with the children and foster parents, usually in conjunction with the regular workers, as required for planning and for mutual understanding of the special worker's role in particular case situations. In cases of children returned to their natural parents or other relatives during the study period, in which the special workers were involved prior to the children's discharge from foster care, the special workers also took responsibility for aftercare casework service for the children and their families.

The first cases selected for the special workers were those with the greatest potential for return to the natural parents, except for cases in which the regular workers had already established a strong relationship with the parents. The special workers later took on cases in which the potential for return home was not high, but which needed work with the natural parents to reach an alternate long-term plan for the children.

Since most of the parents in the selected cases had not been seen with any frequency by the regular agency workers, the special workers approached them with the frank admission that the parents had not been given the consideration their circumstances warranted. The focus was on their problems and concerns, many of which were exclusive of their children in foster care. The parents, almost without exception, were receptive to this approach.

The cases of 37 children from 24 different families in the study sample were handled by the special workers. This is exclusive of cases taken on by the workers for services outside of their project functions, such as supervision of some children in foster care, intake contacts with parents, transportation of foster children to medical facilities, etc. These extra functions were taken on largely toward the end of the project, when the special workers found time beyond their project cases for such activities.

The process of selecting cases for the special workers uncovered an interesting subgroup of mothers who were similar to one another in the circumstances leading to the placement of their children in foster care. In each instance the placement was preceded by a breakup in their relationships with their spouses or conjugal partners. These breakups were closely followed by or almost simultaneous with physical or emotional breakdowns, which sometimes required hospitalization. There was also a pattern of efforts to obtain substitute or supportive help with their child care responsibilities via relatives or friends, but these informal resources were either not available or inadequate.

The circumstances of these women at the time the special workers began working with them could best be described as alienated and extremely isolated. They felt guilty and relatively powerless in their relationships to their children in foster care. They were not sure of their rights, their "worthiness" or ability to take their children back home, or, in some instances, even to visit them regularly.

What became clear was that these women had high potential for taking their children back if given the right kinds of supports in the community. Help with housing, child care and employment could obviously benefit them, but they also clearly gained from the emotional support provided by the caseworkers. Because of their social isolation, some of them needed more than the casework support, and this suggested the need for an ongoing group experience outside the home. The special workers attempted to make referrals to agencies and clinics with group programs or treatment, but these were usually not available or accessible. If it had not been for geographic barriers, it might have been possible to form a group made up specifically of these mothers. This specialized type of group is something that agencies with sufficient numbers of such parents might consider in their program plans.

It should be noted that the women described here were only a subgroup from the total group of parents and other relatives with whom the special workers were concerned. There were only eight, and they were identified mostly by one of the two special workers who worked basically within a unit covering urban Providence. The other worker operated in a more mixed urban, suburban and rural area. The reason the subgroup was singled out for separate description was that the women showed high potential for resuming care of their children, and were the kinds of mothers who might turn up in the caseloads of most agencies of substantial size.

Although this subgroup of mothers surfaced early in the special worker case selection process, it would be incorrect to say that the total group of cases selected was characterized by separated or unattached and socially isolated mothers. In fact, 11 of the 37 children in the special worker cases had both parents in the household at the time of placement. Two other children came from households with fathers and other relatives, two from households with mothers and other relatives, and four from households with other adults only. Almost half (18) of the children in the special workers' caseloads came from households with mothers only, but this proportion was not significantly different from that of the rest of the study sample.

There were no significant differences between the special worker cases and the rest of the sample on the children's age, race, sex, total well-being, or reason for placement, but differences were found on a number of other variables. Significantly ($p < .001$) more children (20 or 54%) in the special worker cases had been in foster care over $1\frac{1}{2}$ years than in the rest of the sample (92 or 25%). This is probably not a function of the selection process of the special workers, but a result of the fact that relatively fewer new placement cases were located in or admitted to the third segment of the study. In all likelihood the special the special workers would have selected such new cases with high potential had they been available.

There was a significant difference between the special worker cases and the others in the frequency of the mother's recent contact with the child in the foster care facility (p < .01). Of the 37 children in the special worker cases, 25, or 70%, were visited at least once a month by the mothers, as compared with 131, or only 42%, of the rest of the sample children. The figures for "no contact at all" were 14% and 34%, respectively, thus favoring the children in cases handled by the special workers. This was probably due to the selection process used by the special workers, the visiting patterns of the mothers being reflective of greater motivation and potential.

Some other variables reflected a greater potential on the part of the mothers in the special worker cases. These were adjustment and behavioral variables based on regular agency caseworkers' judgments on scales in the Baseline Data Form. No significant differences were found in the children, fathers or total family situations of the special worker cases as compared with the others, but there were significant differences on the mother's emotional adjustment (p < .01), behavior of the mother (p < .01), and the mother's supervision and guidance of the child just prior to placement (p < .001).

These variables were scored on three-step scales of "no problem," "moderate problem," and "severe problem." It was in the "severe problem" categories that the differences between the special worker cases and the rest of the sample were most prominent. Thus, about one-third of the special worker cases had mothers with severe emotional problems, but about half of the mothers in the rest of the study sample were so classified. The proportions on behavior of mother showed 19% with severe problems in special worker cases, as compared with 42%

in the others, and the proportions on mother's supervision and guidance of the child were 27% with severe problems in special worker cases, as compared with 49% in the others. More cases in the special worker group showed moderate problems on these three variables. Very few cases in either group were classified as "no problem." In effect, it was a matter of moderate versus severe problems, and the mothers in the special worker cases came out significantly better on that breakdown.

Another variable on which there was a significant difference between the special worker cases and the others was the regular agency worker's projected plan for the child at the time the child entered the project, as shown in Table 3.12.

Table 3.12

Worker's Plan for the Child, by Special Worker Cases Versus All Others

Worker's Plan	Special Worker		Not Special Worker	
	#	%	#	%
No plan as yet	7	19	129	34
Return to parents	26	70	105	28
Permanent foster care	4	11	109	29
Adoption	--	--	26	7
Placement with relatives	--	--	1	< 0.5
Specialized placement	--	--	6	2
Total	37	100	376	100

$x^2 = 28.78$, 3 df, p < .001

None of the worker's plans was projected by the special workers themselves, but it was expected that the purposive selection process would lead to the kind of distribution of cases shown in Table 3.12: the plan for 70% of the cases selected for the special workers was return to parents, as compared with only 28% for the rest of the sample.

Activities of Special Workers

In addition to the characteristics of the cases handled by the special workers, we were interested in how the cases were handled. To get a picture of the service process, the special workers filled out a Monthly Service Schedule. This was intended to obtain data on the number of inperson and telephone contacts with the parents, children, foster parents, other relatives, and collaterals in their caseloads. It also provided for information on the services provided by the agency or other agencies to the clients during the month, particularly those services initiated or arranged for by the special workers.

Another part of the Schedule consisted of the Caseworker's Activity Log, in which the workers noted the dates, time, places, persons contacted, major areas of discussion, and the primary casework techniques used in service interviews. Space was allowed on the Schedules for brief descriptions of the substance of these contacts. The pattern of inperson contacts by the special workers is shown in Table 3.13.

In reviewing this table, it should be recalled that there were 24 families for the 37 children in the special worker caseloads, and the period of service by the workers in these cases ranged from 2 to 11 months. The salient features of Table 3.13 are that the mothers were the persons most frequently contacted by the special workers, as was intended, and that the children were the next most frequently seen. The foster parents were seen in some cases, but with relatively few contacts, probably of an introductory or exploratory nature.

Table 3.13

Number of Inperson Contacts and Persons Contacted
by Special Workers

Number of Contacts	Person Contacted					
	Mother	Father	Child	Other Relative	Foster Mother	Foster Father
1 - 4	6	4	8	5	10	4
5 - 9	4	2	3	--	1	--
10 - 14	3	--	2	--	--	--
15 - 19	3	--	2	1	--	--
20 - 24	2	--	--	--	--	--
25 - 29	2	--	--	--	--	--
Total	20	6	15	6	11	4

The special workers reported a full range of services provided to the clients by the host agency or others, including financial assistance, medical service, etc., as well as services specifically initiated or arranged for by the special workers, including vocational training, legal service, group counseling, psychological testing and recreational service.

Given the pattern of inperson contacts reported in Table 3.13, it was not surprising to find that the major subjects of discussion in the direct contacts by the special workers were the following, in order of frequency: 1) the mother's parental functioning, 2) mother's emotional functioning, 3) child's school functioning, 4) child's emotional functioning, and 5) the sources and adequacy of family income. The mother's parental functioning was far ahead in frequency, being the major subject of discussion in 29% of all inperson contacts, while the mother's emotional functioning was primary in 18% of all contacts. The other three areas of discussion were primary in considerably fewer contacts, 8%, 7% and 6%, respectively. Since the mothers were the most frequently contacted persons, and the children second, these rankings seem consistent. The other major subjects of discussion ranged over 14 other areas of family and individual functioning, none of which exceeded 4% of all contacts.

In a study of services to children in their own homes, the three public child welfare agencies in the study also showed mother's parental functioning and mother's emotional functioning ranking first and second in order of frequency as the most important subjects of discussion in casework interviews.[6] However, in that study the third, fourth and fifth ranked areas were: mother's use of formal resources, mother's physical functioning, and mother's emotional care of the child, respectively. It should be kept in mind that the services-in-own-home study cases were nonplacement cases by definition, while the majority of contacts made by the special workers in the present study occurred while the children were in placement, although there were some aftercare services to children in their own homes.

Another area of interest for comparative purposes was the predominant casework service techniques used by the special workers in their dealings with the mothers and children. These techniques were identified by an adapted form of Hollis's classification of casework treatment.[7] The special worker had to specify which

---

6. Sherman et al., op. cit., p. 56.

7. Florence Hollis, Casework: A Psychosocial Therapy (New York: Random House, 1964).

of the following techniques was the predominant (most important) one in each direct service contact: 1) exploration (obtaining information about present or past situation); 2) structuring (establishing case and procedural expectations with clients); 3) support (emotional support, reassurance and encourgement); 4) directive techniques (advice, recommendations, suggestions, etc.); 5) reflective techniques (client insight-oriented); 6) practical help (concrete help in the form of transportation, goods, escort, etc.); and 7) "other" (including nonverbal or play techniques with young children, or any other activity that did not fit in the other technique categories).

This classification system had been used in the services-in-own-home study, so it is possible again to compare the special worker service activities with those of the workers from the three public welfare agencies in that study. Table 3.14 gives the comparative figures for the two studies.

Table 3.14

Predominant Casework Techniques Used in
Inperson Contacts, Special Project Workers and
Workers From Other Public Agencies

| Casework Technique | Percent of Contacts and Rank | | | |
| | Special Workers | | Other Public Agencies* | |
	%	Rank	%	Rank
Exploration	24	2	23	2
Structuring	11	4.5	12	4
Support	26	1	28	1
Directive techniques	21	3	14	3
Reflective techniques	4	6	11	5.5
Practical help	11	4.5	11	5.5
Other	3	7	1	7
Total	100		100	

*Source: Service to Children in Their Own Homes, p. 59.

The ranking by relative frequency of the techniques used by the special workers in this study and those used by public child welfare agency workers from the prior CWLA study are very similar. It was noted in the earlier study that the predominant use of support as a technique was significantly related to positive outcome of agency service. Support as the predominant technique was also ranked first in frequency for the special workers in this study. Although directive techniques ranked third in both studies, the special workers tended to use them somewhat more frequently than did the own-home service workers.

What was the outcome of special worker services? In one sense this question is misapplied. The design of this study was such that the effectiveness of the special worker strategy was not to be measured only by the outcomes in the cases handled directly by the special workers. It was to be measured in terms of the whole study segment to which the special workers were assigned. It was thought not only that the special workers themselves would bring about the implementation of definite plans, but that they and their activities would have a spin-off effect on other workers in the same segment. Not only could they serve as "in-house advocates" for the natural parents, but in the case review and selection process with other workers the potential for return to parents or some other definite plan could be brought to the attention of the other workers, who might be able to implement the plans themselves. Parenthetically, there was some evidence of initial reluctance or protectiveness on the part of some regular agency workers about their foster children and foster home cases. Most of this pro-tectiveness changed into an active interest in pursuing further work with natural parents in cases they saw as having potential as a result of the review and selection process.

The outcomes or final disposition on the cases handled by the special workers are presented with comparative figures for the rest of the study sample in Table 3.15, but it should be noted that the figures presented in it were not intended for tests of significance for comparative effectiveness, since the small numbers, as well as the study design, rule that out.

Table 3.15

Final Disposition of Study Children in Cases Handled
by Special Workers and Those Handled by
All Others

Final Disposition	Special Worker		Not Special Worker	
	#	%	#	%
No plan implemented	23	62	290	77
Return to parents	7	19	68	18
Permanent foster care	5	14	11	3
Adoption	--	--	1	< 0.5
Placement with relatives	2	5	3	1
Specialized placement	--	--	3	1
Total	37	100	376	100

Recognizing the small numbers involved, although there were proportionally more special worker cases in which definite plans were implemented (38% to 23% for the others), the proportions of children returned to their parents for both groups were almost the same. The expectation was that proportionally more of the special worker children would have returned to their parents. On the other hand, proportionally more permanent foster care plans were implemented by the special workers than by the others. In Table 3.12 it can be seen that permanent foster care plans had been projected for four children from the special worker cases, and plans were actually implemented for five children. In the cases handled by all other workers, permanent foster care had been projected for 109, or 29% of the children, yet it was implemented for only 11 children, or 3%.

These quantitative comparisons are not too meaningful, as has been mentioned. There are some qualitative differences, in that there was considerably more planfulness and service contact involved in the implementation of definite plans by the special workers than in many cases handled by others. This is not to say that there was no comparable quality of work or planfulness by the other workers, but that there were no situations of unplanned or unserviced returns to parents or relatives in the special workers' cases. This is reflected in the fact that none of the children returned to their parents or discharged to other relatives by the special workers had to reenter foster care during the life of the project. The test for the effectiveness of the special worker strategy, as well as the case monitoring approach, is covered in the next chapter.

CHAPTER 4

HOW THE CHILDREN FARED

This chapter is devoted to an analysis of the effect of the different intervention strategies on the foster care status of the children, i.e., whether the status changed from one of "drift" or limbo to a definite plan either in or out of foster care. There is also consideration of how the children fared as a result of the change or lack of change in their foster care status.

The Intervention Strategies and Changes in Foster Care Status

The primary measure of the effect of the intervention strategies involves a comparison of the three segments at the end of the project period in terms of the proportions of children whose status changed from an indeterminate one to an implemented determinate one. Since all the children had an indeterminate status when admitted into the study sample, and the experimental programs were directed toward changing this status, it would be expected ideally that significantly more children in the two experimental segments would have an implemented plan at the end of the project. Table 4.1 gives the breakdown in terms of the disposition at the end of the project.

There are several noteworthy features of Table 4.1. The central one is that there were not significantly more children removed from limbo ("no plan implemented") in either of the two experimental segments than in the control segment ($X^2 = 1.40$, 2 df, NS). In fact, there were proportionally more for whom definite plans were implemented in the control segment (28%) than in the monitoring-only segment (23%) or in the special worker segment (21%). Although the differences in these proportions are not statistically significant, the fact that they are in a direction opposite to the expected one is noteworthy. This result is due to the fact that a higher proportion of the control-group children returned to their parents (again, not significantly more: $x^2 = 4.21$, 2 df, NS). Fewer of the control-group children, on the other hand, were removed from limbo via an alternate plan than in the two experimental segments.

Table 4.1

Final Disposition, by Study Segment

Disposition	Study Segment							
	1 Control		2 Monitoring Only		3 Special Worker		Total	
	#	%	#	%	#	%	#	%
No plan implemented	100	72	114	77	99	79	313	76
Return to parents	32	23	27	18	16	13	75	18
Permanent foster care	4	3	6	4	6	5	16	4
Adoption	1	1	--	--	--	--	1	< 0.5
Return to other relatives	--	--	2	1	3	2	5	1
Specialized placement	1	1	--	--	2	2	3	1
Total	138	100	149	100	126	100	413	100

To get a clearer picture of this finding, an analysis of the effect of the important variable of time in current foster care on the implementation of definite plans was undertaken. A three-way cross-tabulation of time in placement up to the point of the final disposition, final disposition, and study segment provided the data presented in Table 4.2.

Table 4.2

Length of Time in Foster Care, by Final Disposition
and by Study Segment

Length of Time in Foster Care	No Plan Implemented			Return to Parents			Permanent Foster Care			Adoption			Return to Other Relatives			Specialized Placement		
	Study Segment--# of children																	
	1	2	3	1	2	3	1	2	3	1	2	3	1	2	3	1	2	3
Under 3 months	-	-	-	5	15	1	-	-	-	-	-	-	-	-	-	-	-	-
3 to 6 months	8	6	4	3	3	-	-	-	-	-	-	-	-	-	-	-	-	-
6 mos. to 1 year	16	29	17	11	3	4	-	-	-	-	-	-	-	1	1	-	-	2
1 to 1½ years	12	10	5	9	3	3	4	-	1	-	-	-	-	-	-	-	-	-
1½ to 2 years	21	17	15	1	-	5	-	2	-	-	-	-	-	-	-	1	-	-
2 to 3 years	26	28	40	3	1	2	-	4	3	1	-	-	-	1	2	-	-	-
3 to 4 years	17	24	18	-	2	1	-	-	2	-	-	-	-	-	-	-	-	-
Total	100	114	99	32	27	16	4	6	6	1	-	-	-	2	3	1	-	2

Table 4.2 illustrates a point that has been found repeatedly in foster care research--i.e., the shorter the time in foster care the greater the probability of returning home. All 21 children in care under 3 months returned home, but only three of the 64 in care at least 3 years did so. It should be noted that the majority of the children who returned to their parents from the control segment and from the monitoring-only segment were in care less than a year, even though there were more children in care over a year in both those segments. This is consistent with findings from other studies. However, the special worker segment does not show the same breakdown. This is because the control and monitoring segments received by far the largest number of new placements during the project. Given the greater likelihood of return to parents among

newer cases, the special worker segment in effect did not have an equal chance to show as many returns. As a group the children in the special worker segment had been in foster care a significantly longer time, as reported in Chapter 3.

The alternate plans tended to be implemented in cases in which the children had been in foster care for considerably longer time than had the children returned to their natural parents. This makes sense in that it presumably takes time to implement these alternate plans, as well as to be sure that return to the parents is not a viable possibility.

The issue of the time it takes to implement a plan raised the question of how planful the returns to parents had been, particularly the returns after a brief placement period. This involves questions of whether housing, income, physical and mental health of the parents, and child-rearing attitudes and practices were adequate for the return of a child in a planful way--i.e., that it was mutually determined by parents and caseworker that the time and circumstances were right for the child's return and that such return was in the interests of his welfare.

To determine the planfulness of the returns to parents, the caseworkers were asked to indicate on a special form whether the time and place of the child's release were in accord with the casework plan. They were requested to check one of the following alternatives:

    _____ Yes (both time and place in accord with casework plan)
    _____ No, place not in accord with plan (e.g., returned to parents' home instead of adoptive home)
    _____ No, time not in accord with plan (e.g., returned before needed changes in family and/or child took place)
    _____ No, neither time nor place in accord with plan

The point might be raised that there is nothing sacrosanct about a casework plan, that it is more in the mind of the worker than in the mind of parent or child, but it is clear that where the return was contrary to the best judgment of worker or agency, the return was not planful in that it was not mutually determined and agreed upon by the central parties.

In less than half the cases (45%) were the returns to parents in accord with the casework plan. Most of the other cases involved situations where the workers felt it was either too soon (conditions that led to placements were not yet corrected) or the parents were not capable of taking care of the children at home. Because most of these placements were voluntary, the right of the parents to take their children back home had to be respected.

The large proportion of returns that were not in accord with casework plans naturally affects the comparison of the three study segments, which were set up in part to see the effect of planful strategies on the rates of return home. When the segments are compared, taking into account the issue of accord with casework plan, the cases in which children were returned to their parents were distributed as shown in Table 4.3.

Table 4.3

Accordance of Return to Parents With Casework Plan,
by Study Segment

Return in Accord With Casework Plan?	Study Segment							
	1 Control		2 Monitoring		3 Special Worker		Total	
	#	%	#	%	#	%	#	%
Yes	13	42	11	41	9	56	33	45
No	18	58	16	59	7	44	41	55
Total	31	100	27	100	16	100	74*	100

x^2 = 1.13, 2 df, NS

*N = 74 instead of 75 because the casework accord form was not submitted on one case in the control segment.

The noteworthy feature of Table 4.3 is that the majority, although a small one, of the children in the special worker segment were returned home in accordance with the casework plan, while the majority of children in the other two segments were returned contrary to the casework plan. It should be noted that the fact that a return to parents was not in accord with the casework plan does not necessarily mean that the plan precluded ultimate return to parents. It may only have been that the timing or the immediate circumstances of the return were not in accord with the plan. Although the difference between the special worker segment and the other two segments on the accord issue was not statistically significant, probably because of the relatively small numbers involved, it is possibly indicative of somewhat more planfulness in the return of children in special worker cases. In the special worker segment six of the nine children returned in accordance with the plan were from cases handled by the two special workers themselves, whereas only one of the seven returns that were not in accord with casework plans was handled by a special worker.

Although there was some evidence of more planfulness in the return of children to parents in cases handled by special workers, even with control for the fact that the special worker segment had more difficult cases to move by virtue of their being in foster care longer, it is clear that the strategy of using special workers did not lead to significantly more returns to parents or to the implementation of definite plans in general. Consideration is given later in this analysis to the ramifications of this finding, but the finding is clear from a statistical point of view.

What of the other strategy of monitoring cases via the quarterly reports? The data given in Table 4.1 make it apparent that this strategy was no more successful by itself or in conjunction with the special worker strategy than the regular practice represented in the control segment. One may speculate about reasons

for this finding, one of which is the possibility of a Hawthorne effect. The
staff of the control segment, after all, knew it was under scrutiny in terms of
the goals of the project. However, there was one finding that would tend to
rule out the Hawthorne effect as an explanation. This finding came to light
through a comparison of the distributions of children in each segment on the
worker's projected plans for them at the beginning of the project or at the time
of placement, and at the end of the project or at the time of discharge. Table
4.4 gives these distributions.

Table 4.4

Caseworker's Plan for the Child Before
and After Project Intervention, by Study Segment

Caseworker's Plan	Study Segment											
	1 Control				2 Monitoring				3 Special Worker			
	Before		After		Before		After		Before		After	
	#	%	#	%	#	%	#	%	#	%	#	%
No plan as yet	64	46	11	8	25	17	12	8	47	37	10	8
Return to parents	26	19	39	28	63	42	23	15	42	33	37	29
Permanent foster care	45	33	45	33	36	24	48	32	32	25	47	37
Adoption	1	< 0.5	5	4	23	15	29	20	2	2	4	3
Placement with relatives	--	--	--	--	1	1	--	--	--	--	--	--
Specialized placement	2	1	--	--	1	1	2	1	3	2	1	1
Not applicable --definite plan implemented	--	--	38	28	--	--	35	23	--	--	27	21
Total	138	100	138	100	149	100	149	100	126	100	126	100

The salient feature of the distributions in Table 4.4 is the sharp decrease in the proportions of children for whom the plan is return to parents in the monitoring and special worker segments when the before and after figures are compared. This is accompanied by a sharp increase in the proportions of children slated for permanent foster care. This marked shift in plans did not occur in the control segment. What apparently happened was that the workers held accountable by the monitoring procedure in segments 2 and 3 tended to become less optimistic about projecting return to parents as a viable plan and more likely to opt for permanent foster care. The workers in the control segment, who were not required to make a quarterly accounting of their efforts and progress toward implementing return home plans, became more rather than less optimistic in their projections about return to parents.

This impression was borne out when the initial and final plans for the children were checked out on a case-by-case basis, in contrast to the straight comparison of the before and after distributions given in Table 4.4. Of the 46 children for whom no definite plans had been decided upon at the start of the project year, but for whom return home was the final plan, 26, or over half, were from the control segment. In other words, significantly more return home plans were projected for the control group cases by the end of the project than for the two segments using the monitoring form. It is also noteworthy that in only two cases from the control segment were plans changed from return home to permanent foster care, whereas in 19 cases from the monitoring and special worker segments (9 and 10, respectively) the plans were changed from return home to permanent foster care. Although the numbers are small, their disproportions are large enough to suggest the same overall trend toward more conservative estimates of return to parents in the cases with monitoring-form accountability than in cases in the control segment. All of this indicates that the monitoring form had an effect as an intervention strategy, but its effect represented more of a change in form (projected plans) than substance (implemented plans).

Factors Associated With the Implementation of Definite Plans

The fact that the experimental variables or intervention strategies did not show a statistically significant relationship to the implementation of definite plans led us to analyze the relationship of certain antecedent variables to the implementation of plans. The purpose of this analysis was to see whether any of these variables might be more important than the experimental variables in explaining variation in outcomes.

The analysis of antecedent variables amounted mostly to a study of their effect on the rate of return to parents, since return to parental home accounted for 75 of the 100 children who were removed from the limbo of temporary foster care. Since the alternate plans accounted for relatively few cases in the sample, they were of only peripheral importance from a statistical point of view. Consequently, they are all combined into an "Alternate Plan" category in the following analysis. However, if any of the alternate plans shows marked divergence from the others, this is mentioned.

Several other studies have indicated that certain antecedent variables are related to the continuance in and duration of foster care. Jenkins found that the child's age, ethnic group, and reason for placement, among others, were significantly related to duration of foster care.[1] Murphy found that the mother's age at placement of the child also had a strong nonlinear relationship to the duration of foster care.[2] Like Jenkins, Fanshel found that there was

---

1. Shirley Jenkins, "Duration of Foster Care: Some Relevant Antecedent Variables," Child Welfare, XLVI (October 1967), pp. 450-455.

2. H.B.M. Murphy, "Predicting Duration of Foster Care," Child Welfare, XLVII (February 1968), pp. 76-84.

considerable variation in the percentage of children leaving foster care during the first year after entry according to the reason for placement.[3]

These and other demographic variables were analyzed in relation to final disposition, as were other adjustment and functioning variables based upon caseworker assessments of children and parents at the start of the project. One variable already alluded to that we knew to be important in relation to final disposition was the amount of time spent in foster care by the child prior to entrance into the study. The relationship of time in foster care at the point of admission to the study to the final disposition is shown in Table 4.5.

Table 4.5

Length of Time in Foster Care, by Final
Disposition of the Case

Length of Time in Care	Final Disposition							
	No Plan Implemented		Return to Parents		Alternate Plan		Total	
	#	%	#	%	#	%	#	%
Under 3 months	90	70	35	27	3	2	128	100
3 to 6 months	16	55	8	28	5	17	29	100
6 months to 1 year	54	74	16	22	3	4	73	100
1 year to 1½ years	61	86	9	13	1	1	71	100
1½ years to 2 years	32	78	1	2	8	20	41	100
2 years to 2½ years	33	80	3	7	5	12	41	100
2½ years to 3 years	27	90	3	10	--	--	30	100
Total	313	76	75	18	25	6	413	100

---

3. David Fanshel, "The Exit of Children From Foster Care: An Interim Research Report," Child Welfare, L (February 1971), pp. 65-80.

The effect of length of time in foster care at the end of the project on return
to parents was portrayed earlier in Table 4.2 in conjunction with the intervention strategies and their effect on outcome or final disposition. When length
of time in care at the _start_ of the project (as illustrated in Table 4.5) is
examined in relation to final disposition, there is again a strong, statistically
significant relationship ($K_X2 = 18.37, 2$ df, $p < .001$) between time in care and
return to parents.[4]

When the effect of time in care on _all_ implemented plans (including "Return to
Parents" and "Alternate Plans") is tested, the relationship is still statistically
significant ($K_X2 = 10.79$, 2 df, $p < .01$), but not so strong as the relationship
between time in care and return to parents. This is because over half of the
alternate plan cases involved children who had been in care at least 1 year,
whereas a large majority of the return-to-parents cases (79%) involved children
who had been in care _under_ 1 year at the start of the project. As noted earlier,
by their very nature alternate care plans require the passage of time, if only
to rule out the possibility of return to parents.

Reason for Placement

Findings by other investigators of a strong relation of discharge from foster
care to the original reason for placement led us to analyze this phenomenon
in this sample. The reasons for placement given in Table 4.6 were grouped to
make them somewhat similar, insofar as possible, to the groupings or classification of reasons used by the investigators.

---

4. The Komolgorov-Smirnov Two-Sample Test with chi-square approximation (K_X2)
was used to test for significant difference between "No Plan Implemented" distribution and "Return to Parents" distribution. It should be noted that this test
always has two degrees of freedom regardless of the number of ranks in the distributions. See Hubert Blalock, _Social Statistics_ (New York: McGraw-Hill,
1960), p. 205.

Table 4.6

Reason for Placement, by Final Disposition of the Case

Reason for Placement	No Plan Implemented #	No Plan Implemented %	Return to Parents #	Return to Parents %	Alternate Plan #	Alternate Plan %	Total #	Total %
Parent's Emotional Problem or Mental Illness	102	77	23	17	8	6	133	100
Neglect or Abuse of Child	70	81	7	8	9	10	86	100
Parent Unwilling to Care for Child	52	74	13	19	5	7	70	100
Family Problem	28	78	5	14	3	8	36	100
Antisocial Behavior of Parent	19	86	3	14	--	--	22	100
Environmental Problems (financial need or inadequate housing)	14	70	6	30	--	--	20	100
Child's Emotional or Behavioral Problem	10	56	8	44	--	--	18	100
Parent's Physical Illness or Disability	8	53		47	--	--	15	100
Other (physical handicap or mental retardation of child; death of caretaking parent; employment of caretaking parent)	10	77	3	23	--	--	13	100
Total	313	76	75	18	25	6	413	100

The largest category consisted of 133 children placed because of the parents' emotional problem or mental illness. Approximately one child in six in this group returned home, a rate close to that for children placed because of parents' unwillingness to care for them.

A noteworthy feature of Table 4.6 is that significantly ($x^2 = 5.67$, 1 df, $p < .02$) fewer of the children from the neglect and abuse category were returned to their parents than of children from the other categories. The neglect and abuse category was also the only one in which an alternate plan was provided for more children than were returned to their parents. Thus, children placed because of neglect and abuse appear from this sample to have the least relative likelihood of returning to their parents. This is somewhat at odds with Fanshel's findings that the child's behavior problem as the reason for placement has the lowest percentage of children leaving foster care.[5] Jenkins also found that "child's problems," as compared with "physical illness of mother," "mental illness of mother," "neglect and abuse," and "family problems," had disproportionately more children with longer duration in foster care.[6]

The children in this study who were placed primarily because of their own emotional or behavior problems did not do badly in terms of return to parents (eight out of 18 returning within the study period) relative to children who were placed for other reasons. However, their number was small in the sample, as was that of those placed because of physical illness or disability of the caretaking parent. The latter group, too, came off relatively well (seven out of 15 children returned to parents), which is consistent with findings from the other studies. This group would have been more impressive numerically if we had not excluded the brief shelter-care cases from the sample. Those cases include many children placed because of the physical illness of the caretaking parent and returned to the parents rather quickly when the illness or hospitalization ended. Other

---

5. Fanshel, op. cit., p. 73.
6. Jenkins, op. cit., p. 455.

sampling exclusions used in this study might well be responsible for some of the differences from other studies on return rates based on reason for placement.

Demographic Characteristics

Turning to demographic variables and their relationships to the final disposition of the cases in this study, some of the findings correspond with those from other studies of foster care and some do not. Like Jenkins, we found that household composition of the natural family had no bearing on the frequency of return home. Children with both parents in the household showed a return rate of 20%, as against 21% for the children who had only one parent in the household.

The adequacy of the housing of the natural parents in terms of space and facilities was found to be significantly related to the return of children to their parents. Proportionally more children were returned to parents whose housing was considered "adequate" or at least "marginal" than those whose housing was rated "inadequate" by the workers at the start of the study. A total of 30% of the children whose parents' housing was rated "adequate" and 25% with housing rated as "marginal" were returned home as compared with only 4% with "inadequate" housing. Jenkins had a similar finding about the relationship between type of housing and length of time in care, with significantly more children going home sooner to families with private houses or apartments than those with rooms only.[7] She also found significantly more children going home sooner to parents whose main source of income was public assistance rather than earnings.[8] A similar significant finding occurred in this sample, in which only 12% of the children whose parents were not receiving any public assistance at time of placement were returned home, as compared with 25% for parents receiving full assistance and 35% for parents receiving supplementary assistance.

---

7. Ibid., p. 454.

8. Ibid.

The finding about housing makes sense on the face of it. The agency would be more likely to return a child from foster care to parents who have adequate space and facilities in the home for the child than to those who do not. On the other hand, the finding on public assistance and return home might not make much immediate sense unless one considers that it may be easier for a family already receiving public assistance to obtain the additional assistance needed to enable them to take on the expense entailed in having the child at home again.

Other studies have generated mixed findings about the age of the child placed and the likelihood of early discharge from foster care. Jenkins found a significant relationship between the age of the child at placement and discharge from foster care, with proportionally more children in the younger age groups (under 6 years) in short-term care than those in the older age groups (12 years and over).[9] Fanshel, like Maas and Engler, did not find a relationship between age of the child and exit from foster care.[10] Murphy, too, found that the child's age was not predictive of duration of foster care.[11]

Although this study shows a significant relationship between age of child at placement and final disposition, the relationship is not linear. The younger children (under 3 years) and the older children (7 years and older) showed proportionally larger numbers for whom a definite plan was implemented than did the intermediate age group (between 3 and 7 years). Table 4.7 shows the relationship.

_____

9. Ibid., p. 453.

10. Fanshel, op. cit., p. 69.

11. Murphy, op. cit., p. 77.

Table 4.7

Age of Child at Current Placement and Final
Disposition of the Case

| Age of Child | Final Disposition | | | | | | | |
| | No Plan Implemented | | Return to Parents | | Alternate Plan | | Total | |
	#	%	#	%	#	%	#	%
Under 1 year	53	70	19	25	4	5	76	100
1 to 3 years	86	83	12	12	5	5	103	100
3 to 5 years	62	84	9	12	3	4	74	100
5 to 7 years	46	82	8	14	2	4	56	100
7 to 9 years	32	68	10	21	5	11	47	100
9 to 11 years	26	70	8	22	3	8	37	100
11 to 13 years	8	40	9	45	3	15	20	100
Total	313	76	75	18	25	6	413	100

There is a strong statistical relationship between age and final disposition
(x^2 = 17.22, 2 df, p < .001) when considering all types of implemented plans.
If one tests only the return-home group as compared with the no-implemented-
plan group, the relationship is still statistically significant, but not so
strong (x^2 = 13.64, 2 df, p < .01). This is in part because more permanent
foster care and residential treatment plans were implemented in the older age
group (7 years and older), which, when added to the concentration of children
in that age category who were returned to their parents, strengthened the relationship between age and implemented plans.

Another demographic variable on which there have been mixed findings relative to duration of foster care is ethnicity. Jenkins found a significant relationship between these variables in that significantly more black children had a short duration (under 3 months) of foster care than white or Puerto Rican children.[12] Fanshel, on the other hand, did not find a statistically significant relationship between ethnicity and exit from foster care, although there were somewhat more white and Puerto Rican than black children discharged from foster care.[13] This study also found no significant relationship between ethnicity and return home or implementation of alternate plans, although slightly more black children (22%) than white (17%) returned to their parents during the project.

These mixed findings suggest that whether certain demographic variables are significantly related to duration of foster care may depend on local (community and/or agency) circumstances. The findings in this study concerning the variable of child's sex lends some credence to this interpretation. Whereas Murphy and Fanshel found no significant relationship between sex and exit from foster care, it was found that significantly more boys than girls had definite plans implemented (x^2 = 5.09, 1 df, p < .05) in this project, as shown in Table 4.8.

Table 4.8

Sex of Child, by Final Disposition of the Case

Sex of Child	Final Disposition							
	No Plan Implemented		Return to Parents		Alternate Plan		Total	
	#	%	#	%	#	%	#	%
Male	161	71	50	22	15	6	226	100
Female	152	81	25	13	10	5	187	100
Total	313	76	75	18	25	6	413	100

12. Jenkins, op. cit.

13. Fanshel, op. cit., p. 70.

Proportionally more boys than girls were returned to their parents. The difference between boys and girls returning to their parents relative to no implemented plans is significant (x^2 = 5.06, 1 df, p < .05). If, however, one looks separately at children in foster family care and those placed at the Children's Center, the difference in rate of return home for boys and girls from either setting is slight. Many more boys than girls are admitted to the Children's Center, a short-time facility. So, by controlling for the type of foster care facility, it became apparent that the higher rate of return to parents for boys was more a function of the workings of these agency foster care facilities than a function of difference in the attributes of boys versus girls in this sample.

One further demographic variable was examined in relation to the outcome in these cases because it had been found to be significant by one other investigator. That variable was mother's age at the time of current placement. Murphy had found a trend ". . . with the proportion of children requiring long-term care increasing for mothers in their early 20s, decreasing again . . . in their early 30s, and then increasing again as the mothers approach and exceed the age of 40."[14] No such trend was discernible in this sample of mothers, and there was no significant relationship between their ages and the return of children to them.

Parental Functioning

In addition to the demographic variables reported upon, behavioral and attitudinal characteristics of the natural parents, children and foster parents based on caseworker assessments at the start of the project were analyzed in relation to final disposition. The first dealt with the functioning of the natural mothers in a number of critical areas or roles: child care, marital, homemaking, etc.

---

14. Murphy, op. cit.

The workers rated the mothers in these areas on a three-point scale of "No Pro-blem," "Moderate Problem" and "Severe Problem." The most meaningful break in this scale was between "Severe Problem" on the one hand and "Moderate Problem" or "No Problem" on the other hand when the ratings on these variables were cross-tabulated with final disposition. The following variables showed a significant relationship to return to parents, with "Severe Problem" obviously associated with the smallest numbers of children returned to their parents: mother's marital functioning ($p < .001$), household management ($p < .05$), behavior ($p < .01$), physical care of the child ($p < .001$), emotional care of the child ($p < .001$), and supervision and guidance of the child ($p < .01$).

These same variables also showed a significant relationship to the implementation of all definite plans, with the exception of supervision and guidance of the child. The reason for this exception was that, although children were most unlikely to be returned home if there was a "Severe Problem" in parental guidance and supervision, they were very likely to have alternate plans implemented. This makes sense, in that one would expect plans other than return to parents to be made in cases where the mother exhibited severe problems in guidance and super-vision, but it served to offset the statistical significance of the category for return home.

Two of the variables concerning the mother's functioning turned out not to be significantly related to either return to parents or to the implementation of any definite plan. They were: 1) mother's financial management and 2) mother's emotional adjustment. The workers tended to identify emotional adjustment pro-blems of at least a "moderate" nature in these mothers generally and readily; 93% of the total known group were identified as having "problems." Consequently, since there was little variation on this variable, there was no significant relationship to final disposition. However, when the workers were asked whether the mother exhibited specific <u>behavior</u> (such as excessive drinking, use of drugs, sexual promiscuity, etc.) there was considerably more variation, and the presence of these deviations showed a significant relationship to final disposition, as did the "severe problems" noted previously.

The functioning of the fathers, too, in some of the cited areas showed significant relations with final disposition. Absence of a severe problem in the father's marital functioning was significantly related to return to parents ($p < .01$), as well as to all implemented plans ($p < .01$). Since the father's marital functioning is the complement of the mother's, the similar finding of significance was to be expected. Other areas of father's functioning that were significantly related to return to parents included: his physical care of the child, his emotional care of the child, and supervision and guidance of the child, all at the .02 level of significance. Only his emotional care of the child, however, was significantly related ($p < .05$) to <u>all</u> implemented plans. This, again, was because severe problem cases more frequently eventuated in the implementation of alternate plans. Neither the father's emotional adjustment nor specific behavior problems, as assessed by the workers, were significantly related to final disposition.

The findings of significance concerning marital and child care functioning of both mothers and fathers should be viewed as rather "soft" findings in the sense that workers' assessments in one area of functioning are likely to spill over and affect their ratings in other areas of functioning, thus creating a "halo effect" representing a general impression of the parents, rather than specific variable scores in the areas of functioning. The overall impression of these soft data points to the association of severe child care and marital problems in the natural parents with retention of the children in "temporary" foster care, or at best the implementation of alterante plans (most frequently permanent foster care) rather than return to parents.

Child Behavior and Adjustment

Child adjustment variables based on caseworker assessments at the start of the study were also analyzed in relation to final disposition. The same rating scale of "No Problem," "Moderate Problem" and "Severe Problem" was applied to various areas of the child's functioning. The following variables showed no significant relationship to final disposition, regardless of whether it was return to parents or to any implemented plan: child's family functioning in relation to parents and siblings, school learning problems, physical functioning, behavior and emotional adjustment, and functioning with peers.

There were only two areas in which the child's functioning had a significant relationship to final disposition--his social functioning with adults and his school behavior problems, as distinct from learning problems. These two findings appeared somewhat anomolous because the children who remained in the limbo of foster care with no plan implemented seemed better off than the others. Table 4.9 illustrates this point as far as social functioning with adults is concerned.

Table 4.9

Child's Social Functioning With Adults, by
Final Disposition of the Case

Child's Functioning With Adults	Final Disposition							
	No Plan Implemented		Return to Parents		Alternate Plan		Total	
	#	%	#	%	#	%	#	%
No problem	129	77	30	18	8	5	167	100
Moderate problem	22	67	8	24	3	9	33	100
Severe problem	6	46	5	38	2	15	13	100
Not applicable	123	79	26	17	7	4	156	100
No information	33	75	6	14	5	11	44	100
Total	313	76	75	18	25	6	413	100

One point about Table 4.9 is that there were many children for whom the scale on social functioning was not applicable, largely because they were too young for the item to be meaningful. This reduced considerably the number of cases on which the statistical test of significance was based, but there were significantly more children with problems in their relations with adults in the implemented plan group (return to parents and alternate plans combined) than in the group remaining in limbo ($X^2 = 7.02$, 2 df, $p < .05$).

With regard to the child's school behavior problems, there were significantly more children with school behavior problems who returned to their parents than those who had no plans implemented ($X^2 = 6.18$, 2 df, $p < .05$). There was not a significant difference between the total implemented plan group and the "no plan" group, however. Table 4.10 illustrates much the same trend of fewer problems among the "no plan" group as is illustrated in Table 4.9.

Table 4.10

Child's School Behavior Problem, by Final Disposition

| School Behavior Problem | Final Disposition | | | | | | | |
| | No Plan Implemented | | Return to Parents | | Alternate Plan | | Total | |
	#	%	#	%	#	%	#	%
No problem	48	76	9	14	6	9	63	100
Moderate problem	20	57	11	31	4	11	35	100
Severe problem	13	59	8	36	1	5	22	100
Not applicable	216	79	44	16	12	4	272	100
No information	16	76	3	14	2	10	21	100
Total	313	76	75	18	25	6	413	100

Again, there were many children in the sample for whom the scale on school behavior problems is not applicable because they are too young to be in school. That there were less than half the children for whom the scale applied and on whom there was sufficient information may have a bearing on the somewhat anomolous statistical finding that significantly more children in the group that were returned to their parents had school behavior problems than those who remained in the limbo of foster care, with no definite plans implemented. However, this reduction of the sample could not explain the unexpected findings in both Tables 4.9 and 4.10 of a larger proportion of children with severe problems who were returned to their parents.

Pursuit of an explanation led again to the Children's Center. It was found that four out of five of the children with severe problems in social functioning with adults, and nine out of 13 children with either a moderate or severe problem in this area, who were returned to their parents, had been discharged from institutional care in the Children's Center, rather than from foster family care. It was also found that seven out of eight children with severe school behavior problems, and 15 out of 19 children with either a moderate or severe problem, who were returned to their parents were returned from the Children's Center. As the children in this sample from the Center tended to be older than those in foster family care, problems in relations with adults (teachers and institutional staff) and in school would tend to be more frequent among them. The point is, however, that some children with severe problems in these two areas were returned to their parents and to the community. It was noted earlier that a significantly higher proportion of children returned to parents from the Children's Center than from foster family care. Both the special project workers and the research interviewer had reported that some children with serious problems were being returned to their families from the Children's Center even though the parents were not equipped or ready to handle the problems presented by these children. The special workers and the interviewers were concerned about the lack of planfulness and of followup services in these cases.

The point being made here is that a greater rate of return to parents can be achieved with little time or effort, but the quality or circumstances of those returns can leave much to be desired from the viewpoint of child and family welfare.

Two other child attributes or adjustment variables were examined in relation to final disposition. One was the caseworker's estimate of the child's intelluctual level; the other was the child's "total well-being" (per Weinstein), which was described earlier. Both are general, crude estimates, but caseworker assessments at the extreme ends of the scales, particularly the low or dysfunctional end, could have important ramifications for the longevity and the movement in and out of foster care for the child. This did not turn out to be the case, however. There were no significant differences on the two scales between the children who remained in foster care and those who returned to their parents or had an alternate plan implemented. The percentages of children estimated as below average intelligence, for example, showed 27% for those children who had no definite plan implemented and 29% for those who returned to their parents. Also, the "no plan" group had 18% of the children assessed as markedly or extremely low in total well-being, as compared with 22% for those who returned to their parents. The numerical differences in both instances are slight.

Along with the adjustment variables already analyzed on the basis of assessments made by caseworkers on the Baseline Data Schedule, we also obtained assessments from the caseworkers on the attitudes of the children, their natural parents, and their foster parents toward possible return to the parents or remaining in foster care. We also obtained information on the child's emotional attachment to his natural parents and foster parents. We thought that much of the planning and the implementation of plans for the children would be developed within the nexus of attitudes and attachments of the children, their natural parents and their foster parents. Part of the analysis, then, was directed toward finding out the relationship of these factors to the final disposition of the case.

As to the children's attachments and attitudes, it is clear from Table 4.11 that the more emotionally attached the child is to his natural mother, the more likely it is that he will be returned home. This is not to say that this is a one-way causal relationship; it is probable that children most attached to their mothers have mothers also attached to them and highly motivated to have them return home.

Table 4.11

Child's Attachment to His Mother, by
Final Disposition of the Case

| Child's Attachment | Final Disposition | | | | | | | |
| | No Plan Implemented | | Return to Parents | | Alternate Plan | | Total | |
	#	%	#	%	#	%	#	%
Very strong emotional tie	44	65	23	34	1	1	68	100
Moderately strong	70	76	18	20	4	4	92	100
Slightly weak	50	85	7	12	2	3	59	100
Very weak	34	74	7	15	5	11	46	100
No emotional tie	41	72	9	16	7	12	57	100
Unknown, too young, etc.	74	81	11	12	6	7	91	100
Total	313	76	75	18	25	6	413	100

Although it is perhaps noteworthy that 16 children with very weak or no emotional ties to their mothers were returned to their parents, the bulk of those returned had strong emotional attachments to their mothers, and there was a statistically significant difference between the returns and "no plan" children relative to degree of attachment (x^2 = 10.41, df = 4, p < .05). There was, however, no significant difference between the "no plan" category and all implemented plans, because almost half of the children for whom alternate plans had been implemented had very weak or no emotional ties to their mothers.

It should be noted that there was no significant relationship between the child's attachment to his natural father and final disposition, regardless of whether the disposition was return to parents or any implemented plan. However, the child's attachment to his foster mother and return to parents had a significant relationship, as shown in Table 4.12.

Table 4.12

Child's Attachment to His Foster Mother, by
Final Disposition of the Case

Child's Attachment	Final Disposition							
	No Plan Implemented		Return to Parents		Alternate Plan		Total	
	#	%	#	%	#	%	#	%
Very strong emotional tie	77	79	8	8	13	13	98	100
Moderately strong	143	82	24	14	7	4	174	100
Slightly weak	15	63	7	29	2	8	24	100
Very weak	4	67	2	33	--	--	6	100
No emotional tie	15	83	3	17	--	--	18	100
Unknown, too young, etc.	59	63	31	33	3	3	93	100
Total	313	76	75	18	25	6	413	100

In many respects the findings in Table 4.12 are the converse of those in Table 4.10. In Table 4.12 the smallest proportion of children with very strong attachments to their foster mothers were in the return-to-parents group. The relationship between attachment to foster mother and return to parents is statistically significant ($x^2 = 6.64$, 2 df, p < .05). There is not, however, a significant difference in degree of attachment to foster mother between the no-implemented-plan group and the total group of 100 for whom some plan was implemented. This was because such a high proportion of the alternate-plan children showed a very strong attachment to the foster mother. Ten of the 13 children in the alternate-plan group with very strong attachments were permanent foster care children, as expected.

There was also a significant negative relationship between the child's attachment to his foster father and return home ($x^2 = 7.99$, 2 df, p < .02), and this is of course parallels the finding with regard to the foster mothers. In general terms, the more attached the child is to his foster parents, the less likely he is to return to his natural parents.

Not only did the child's attachments to natural and foster parents have a bearing on the likelihood of his return to parents, but his attitudes and expectations about return from foster care also had significant relationships to the rate of return. Significantly fewer of the children who were described as reluctant to return home did return to their parents and significantly more children who expected to return to their parents soon did so. There is a particularly strong association ($x^2 = 33.69$, 2 df, p < .001) between the child's expectation about return home and its occurrence, as is illustrated in Table 4.13.

Table 4.13

Child's Expectation of Length of Stay in Foster
Care, by Final Disposition of Case

Child's Expectation	Final Disposition							
	No Plan Implemented		Return to Parents		Alternate Plan		Total	
	#	%	#	%	#	%	#	%
Expects to return home soon	7	29	17	71	--	--	24	100
Expects to return but not in immediate future	48	72	17	25	2	3	67	100
Expects to remain in foster care indefinitely	57	78	6	8	10	14	73	100
Too young to have clear expectation	167	80	31	15	11	5	209	100
Unknown	34	85	4	10	2	5	40	100
Total	313	76	75	18	25	6	413	100

Table 4.13 shows that 17 of the 24 children who expected to return home soon were
returned to their parents within the less-than-a-year period of the project.

Natural Parent and Foster Parent Attitudes Toward Child

Turning to the attitudes of the natural parents and foster parents toward the
child, we found that one variable particularly indicative of parental interest,
concern and involvement was the frequency of the natural mother's contact with
the child in foster care in the period just preceding completion of the Baseline
Data Form. Table 4.14 shows the relationship between this variable and the
final disposition of the case.

Table 4.14

Mother's Contact with Child in Foster Care,
by Final Disposition of the Case

Frequency of Contact	Final Disposition							
	No Plan Implemented		Return to Parents		Alternate Plan		Total	
	#	%	#	%	#	%	#	%
At least once a week	9	39	13	57	1	4	23	100
About once in 2 weeks	24	60	13	32	3	8	40	100
About once a month	75	81	17	18	1	1	93	100
Less than once a month	67	82	12	15	3	4	82	100
No contact at all	93	85	7	6	10	9	110	100
Not applicable--child in care less than a month	40	70	13	23	4	7	57	100
No information	5	62	--	--	3	38	8	100
Total	313	76	75	18	25	6	413	100

As may be seen from the table, the children whose mothers visited them frequently in foster care during the period immediately before their entrance into the study were more likely to return home than those who had infrequent visits (x^2 = 39.68, 4 df, p < .001). Given this strong relationship, it is not surprising that the caseworker's assessment of the mother's attitude toward the child's return home is also strongly associated with the occurrence of return to parents. Table 4.15 shows clearly that the children whose mothers were eager for their return were more likely to return home than those whose mothers had mixed or negative feelings (x^2 = 29.15, 4 df, p < .001).

Table 4.15

Mother's Attitude Toward Child's Return Home,
by Final Disposition of the Case

| Mother's Attitude | Final Disposition | | | | | | | |
| | No Plan Implemented | | Return to Parents | | Alternate Plan | | Total | |
	#	%	#	%	#	%	#	%
Eager for child's return	48	59	33	40	1	1	82	100
Moderately interested in return	55	75	18	25	--	--	73	100
Mixed feelings	83	86	9	9	5	5	97	100
Moderately opposed to return	24	96	1	4	--	--	25	100
Strongly opposed to return	32	67	9	19	7	15	48	100
Not applicable (mother deceased, missing, etc.)	18	75	2	8	4	17	24	100
No information	53	83	3	5	8	12	64	100
Total	313	76	75	18	25	6	413	100

As can be seen, in most cases in the return-to-parents group there were positive attitudes among the mothers toward return, whereas in the bulk of the no-plan cases and the alternate-plan cases there were at best mixed or negative attitudes on the part of the mothers toward return. The nine cases of children who returned to their parents even though the mothers were strongly opposed to return at the start of the study represent changes in the mothers' attitudes over time. In several instances the children themselves were eager for return, one of them even running home from the Children's Center, and the mothers professed a change of attitude about the possibility of the return's working out.

The frequency of the father's visits to the child in foster care was not significantly related to final disposition. This was probably because not nearly so
many fathers as mothers were known to be involved in the situation, so that the
number of cases on which the statistical test was based was markedly reduced.
The same situation held true regarding the fathers' attitudes toward return of
the children. There were only 20 fathers in the entire group of 75 children
returned to parents whose attitudes toward return were known. Of those 20, 10
had positive attitudes, five had mixed feelings, and five were opposed. This
did not represent a marked difference from attitudes of fathers in the other
disposition groups.

As expected, the child's attitude toward return home showed a significant relationship to return to parents (X^2 = 11.52, 4 df, p < .05), but not so strong a
relationship as the mother's attitude toward return (significant at .001 level).
This is probably because many of the children, particularly in the group that
returned to the parents, were too young to express a meaningful attitude, and,
additionally, the mothers were obviously in a much better position to facilitate
the return than the children.

Another finding of interest in the attitudinal data concerns the foster parents'
interest in the child's remaining with them. It is to be expected that if foster
parents are reluctant to keep a child or want him removed, the chances are greater
of that child's being returned to the parents, other things being equal (availability
of another appropriate foster care facility, the relative circumstances of the
natural parents, etc.), than the chances of a child whose foster parents want to
keep him permanently or perhaps adopt him. A dominant foster mother has various
ways to discourage both the natural mother and the social worker from returning

a child to his parents, if her attachment to him is strong enough. The relation-ships between the foster mother's interest in the child's remaining in foster care and the final disposition of the study cases are given in Table 4.16.

Table 4.16

Foster Mother's Interest in Child's Remaining in Foster Care,
by Final Disposition of the Case

Foster Mother's Interest in Child's Remaining	No Plan Implemented		Return to Parents		Alternate Plan		Total	
	#	%	#	%	#	%	#	%
Would like to adopt child	36	82	3	7	5	11	44	100
Would like child permanently without adoption	94	82	12	10	9	8	115	100
Child can remain as long as necessary, but not perma-nently	120	78	32	21	2	1	154	100
Reluctant to have child remain any longer	4	57	3	43	--	--	7	100
Insistent on other arrange-ments for child	5	100	--	--	--	--	5	100
Not applicable--child in institution	38	58	24	36	4	6	66	100
No information	16	73	1	5	5	23	22	100
Total	313	76	75	18	25	6	413	100

This table shows some of the trends that might be expected. For example, a somewhat higher proportion of children whose foster mothers wanted to adopt them or to have them remain permanently did remain in foster care than of those whose foster mothers did not have such a strong interest. The difference, however, was not great enough for statistical significance. Conversely, almost half the chil-dren whose foster mothers were reluctant to have them remain returned home.

It is clear that basic human ingredients such as the child's emotional attachment to his natural mother and foster mother, the mother's attitude toward the child's return and her contacts with the child in foster care, as well as the foster parents' attitudes, affect the implementation of plans. Because passage of time is likely to weaken the mutual attachment of mother and child, time itself is strongly related to implementation of alternate plans and inversely related to return home. Yet, for any intervention strategies to overcome the problems that led to placement and the negative attitudes that prolong it, it takes time, a great deal of effort, and probably many more cases than were included in this sample.

The Children Who Returned to Their Parents

The foregoing analysis of the factors associated with final disposition high-lighted the predominance of return to parents among the various implemented plans. This outcome accounted for 75 of the 100 implemented plans and, in the short run at least, it is the most likely alternative to the limbo of extended "temporary" foster care.

Because of its predominance, and because we were able to follow up most of these discharged cases through independent research interviews, it seemed worthwhile to take a more detailed look at them. These 75 cases made up 18% of the total sample of 413 children. It is difficult to know whether this is a high or low rate of return to parents, because comparable figures are hard to come by. Shapiro reported that 28% of the 624 foster care children followed in the Columbia University Child Welfare Research Project in New York City had been discharged within 1 year.[15] However, there are differences in the circumstances of the New York City group and this Rhode Island group. First, this sample had

_____

15. Deborah Shapiro, "Agency Investment in Foster Care: After the First Year," a modified version of a paper presented at Foster Care: A Conference on Research Findings and Implications for Policy and Practice, West Point, New York, October 30, 1972, p. 4. (Mimeographed.)

children in care up to 3 years at the start of the project, whereas the children in the New York sample were all new admissions. Second, there were large numbers of children in "shelter care" in the New York sample, a group that tends to show quicker discharges; shelter care cases were ruled out of this sample.

It should be recalled that a primary reason for the followup interviews was to check on the possibility that some children, in the general push for return to parents under the intervention strategies, might be returned to families who were not ready or able to care for them adequately. One clear indicator of such a possibility would be the need for a child to reenter foster care. The record of each child in the sample who returned to his parents from April 1, 1971, to March 1, 1972 was checked for readmission to foster care up to July 1, 1972. In all, 20 of the 75 children were returned to foster care during the life of the project, and they were fairly evenly distributed over the three segments of the study. So, on the basis of the criterion of return to foster care at any rate, it cannot be said that the experimental groups showed any higher incidence of precipitious or ill-planned returns to parents than the control group.

The figure of 20 out of 75, or 27%, of the children who were discharged to parents having to reenter foster care is also difficult to assess because of lack of comparable figures. Again, the Columbia University Child Welfare Project sheds some light on this. Its figures, however, cover a 5-year span. Within that period only 62 out of 354 children (17.5%) discharged from foster care had to reenter foster care.[16] Although that percentage does not appear large, it is of concern that all of those 62 children had more than one discharge and

16. "Placement Patterns: A Five-Year Analysis of Placements, Replacement and Discharge"--Tables and Charts Prepared by Eugene B. Shinn for Foster Care: A Conference on Research Findings and Implications for Policy and Practice, West Point, New York, October 30, 1972, Table #11. (Mimeographed)

reentry, and some as many as seven, during the 5-year period, for a mean of 3.4 entries per child. This suggests that reentry into foster care is a chronic problem for many children, and it warrants the same serious consideration as has been given to the problem of repeated replacements from one foster care facility to another.

The research interviewer, a highly experienced and professionally trained social worker, had an initial interview with the parents of 50 of the 75 children who returned home. The reasons for not interviewing the parents of the other 25 children were as follows: mother refused to be interviewed--7 children; family moved out of the state--2 children; child returned to foster care before the first interview--3 children; unable to contact mother (relocated, whereabouts unknown, etc.)--7 children; recommendation not to interview (interviewer safety)-- 2 children; and other reasons (mostly agency worker recommendations that client not be interviewed because of tenuous agency relationship with client)--4 children.

One of the more important rating scales on the research interviewer's Initial Interview Schedule dealt with the probability of the child's being able to remain in the parental home. On the basis of her ratings on this scale, the interviewer was able to predict with considerable accuracy which children would have to be returned to foster care and which had a good chance of remaining with their parents. Table 4.17 illustrates this.

As can be seen, none of the five children given a "very good" chance of remaining at home were returned to foster care, and only one of the eight rated as having a "good" chance was returned. Conversely, 10 of the 14 children rated as having either "poor" or "very poor" chances of remaining at home were returned to foster care. When this distribution was dichotomized between those rated as "poor" or "very poor" and all others, the test results were statistically significant (x^2 = 13.27, 1 df, p < .001).

Table 4.17

Interviewer's Rating of Probability of Child's
Remaining at Home, by Child's Final Project Status

| Probability Rating | Child's Final Status | |
	Not Returned to Foster Care	Returned to Foster Care
Very Good	5	--
Good	7	1
50-50	19	4
Poor	2	6
Very Poor	2	4
Total	35	15

Given this accuracy in prediction, we explored with the interviewer the salient factors that entered into her ratings on that particular scale. She described a mix of interpersonal, emotional and environmental factors that went into her thinking. She was especially concerned with the lack of supportive services for a number of families that were clearly in need of them. She identified the crucial needs as housing, financial and health services, together with the emotional support of an agency worker in sustaining these families.

Since we had data available on the Interview Schedule concerning the factors the interviewer had cited, we analyzed them in relation to the child's final project status (remained at home or returned to care). These factors included the mother's functioning in the following areas: relations with child, household management, physical functioning, behavior, emotional adjustment, emotional care of the child, supervision of the child, and marital functioning. The same areas of functioning for the father were also covered, as were items on the child's total well-being and on total family cohesiveness. In addition to these data were some "harder" data on number of children in the household, family status (intact/nonintact), age and sex of the child, and finally, on external factors dealing with housing, income, etc.

From among all these factors the only ones that turned out to be statistically significant were those dealing with the external circumstances of the family, specifically housing and financial problems. Table 4.18 shows the relationship of the external circumstances items from the Interview Schedule and the child's final project status.

Table 4.18

Problems in Family's External Circumstances,
by Child's Final Project Status

| External Problems | Child's Final Status | |
	Not Returned to Foster Care	Returned to Foster Care
None	20	2
Inadequate income	9	8
Housing problem	5	3
Lack of supportive persons (relatives, friends, etc.)	1	1
Other	--	1
Total	35	15

The outstanding fact shown in Table 4.18 is that among the children who were returned to foster care from the families that were interviewed, 13 out of 15 had serious identified problems in their external circumstances that the interviewer thought might interfere with their remaining at home. This compares with only 15 out of the 35 children who were not returned to foster care. The difference was of course statistically significant ($X^2 = 6.50$, 2 df, $p < .02$).

There were several suggestive findings among the other factors assessed by the interviewer concerning the family, but none was statistically significant. Some of these findings were in an unexpected direction. For example, among the interviewed cases children were returned to foster care more frequently from intact families (both parents present) than from single-parent families. Since we had data concerning these factors in the caseworker's Outcome Schedule on all 75 cases of children returned to their parents, we did a further statistical analysis to see whether these factors would show significance with the increased (full) number of cases.

It turned out that significantly more children were returned to foster care from the intact families. Table 4.19 illustrates this finding.

Table 4.19

Parental Household to Which Child Was Returned,
by Child's Final Project Status

Persons in Parental Household	Child's Final Status					
	Not Returned to Foster Care		Returned to Foster Care		Total	
	#	%	#	%	#	%
Mother only	31	84	6	16	37	100
Both parents	8	44	10	56	18	100
Both parents plus other adults	--	--	1	100	1	100
Father only	1	50	1	50	2	100
Mother and other relatives	10	91	1	9	11	100
Mother and nonrelatives	5	83	1	17	6	100
Total	55	73	20	27	75	100

It should be noted that 11 out of the 19 children in households in which both parents were present were returned to foster care, as compared with only seven of 39 children in housholds with single parents (mothers or fathers only) and only two of 17 children in households with mothers and other persons (nonspouses). When a chi-square test was run on these three groupings and the child's final status, the results were statistically significant (X^2 = 12.92, 2 df, p < .01). If we had run the test by the households with both parents versus all other types of household combined, the statistical results would have been even stronger.

This rather anomolous finding may have some substance beyond its statistical significance. The special workers had noted in some of the cases they followed up after discharge that there was tension resulting from the presence of the father or father surrogate in the home, even in cases where the regular agency caseworkers had indicated that the fathers' attitudes were favorable toward the return of the child to the parents' home. These cases were few and not systematically identified, so that statistical tests could not be applied. The findings prompt speculation that it may be more difficult for a child returned from foster care to fit into a parents/child triad than into a parent/child dyad of mother and child only.

Another factor that showed a significant relationship to the child's final project status was the mother's behavior as assessed by the agency caseworker at the time of the child's discharge. This, too, was in a direction not expected, as shown in Table 4.20.

Table 4.20

Caseworker's Assessment of Mother's Behavior
at Discharge, by Child's Final Project Status

Assessment of Mother's Behavior	Child's Final Status					
	Not Returned to Foster Care		Returned to Foster Care		Total	
	#	%	#	%	#	%
No problem	20	62	12	38	32	100
Moderate problem	24	92	2	8	26	100
Severe problem	7	70	3.	30	10	100
Unknown	4	67	2	33	6	100
Not applicable	--	--	1	100	1	100
Total	55	73	20	27	75	100

The anomolous feature of the table is that proportionally more (92%) of the children whose mothers had "moderate" behavior problems remained at home than children whose mothers had no problem (62%). It would be unwise to assume a causal
nature in this finding. First, the relationship of these variables is not so
strong as the prior one between household composition and child's final project
status, and it could have occurred by chance. Second, the finding could be
taken more seriously had there been a disproportionate number of children remaining at home with mothers in the "severe" problem category, but this was not the
case.

There were no findings of significance in the relationship of the other factors
assessed by caseworkers at discharge and the child's final project status. From
examination of these findings from the interviewer schedules, it can be said that
problems in the environmental circumstances of the families had a significant
effect on the child's final project status--a negative effect in that significantly

more children from families with problems in housing, income, etc., were returned to foster care during the project. On the other hand, factors such as behavior problems in the mothers (at least "moderate" problems) and single-parent households clearly did not lead to more frequent return to foster care. If anything, there is some evidence of the opposite being true, so it can be said that the presence of these problems does not by itself lead to children's return to foster care.

The return of a child to foster care can be considered a negative outcome in most instances. And, as other research findings suggest, it may be a chronic problem for those children who experience it. The fact that a child was not returned to foster care during the life of this project was not, however, taken as a positive outcome by itself. In order to judge how well the children fared who remained at home, the research interviewer carried out followup interviews at about 4 months after her initial postdischarge interview in the cases of any children who had not been returned to foster care. On the basis of these interviews she assessed the circumstances and functioning of the families and children at that time.

Each of the items from the Initial Interview Schedule was repeated in the Final Interview Schedule, and the interviewer was asked to rate whether the individual or family had improved, showed no change, or had got worse in each of the areas since the first interview. Generally speaking, without having had the advantage of seeing the statistical results, the interviewer at the time of her initial interview was not sanguine about a number of the children and their families. However, at the time of her second interview she found more to be hopeful about and saw signs of either positive change or stability that she had not expected.

The statistical findings tend to bear out her impressions. First, the mean rating of changes in the child's functioning was statistically significant ($p < .05$) and in a positive direction. The global rating of the "child's total well-being" also showed a positive change that was statistically significant ($p < .05$). The interviewer's rating of family cohesion did not show a significant change in either direction. The mean ratings of changes in the mother's functioning, the father's functioning, and in the external circumstances of the family showed positive trends, but no one of them was large enough to be statistically significant. However, the overall mean rating of changes in the case (child, mother, father and external circumstances) was statistically significant ($p < .01$), because the direction of change in all the components was positive.

On the basis of these findings it can be said that retention of children with their parents after discharge from foster care is much to be desired, and return to foster care is much to be avoided, if possible. This strongly suggests the need for followup services to provide for these families environmental and emotional supports to sustain the child in the family and thus prevent the all-too-frequent chronic cycle of discharge-return-discharge. The evidence in these followup interviews indicates that many of these families can be sustained and can improve, even after shaky starts at the time of the child's discharge from foster care.

The Children Who Received Alternate Care

Because 75% of all implemented plans during the project were return to parents, our procedure was to lump together the 25 alternative plan cases, for ease and economy of tabular presentation. Although not numerically impressive, these plans and the children to whom they applied do require some individual analysis and description.

The first of the alternatives to be considered is adoption. By the end of the project only one child fit the study criteria of an implemented adoption plan, i.e., placement in an adoptive home from foster care and the legal surrender of parental rights required for such a placement. This was an infant boy on whom the surrender was obtained and who was transferred from a temporary foster family home into an adoptive home.

Not too much should be made of the fact that only one adoptive plan was implemented. It should be recalled that children on whom legal surrenders had already been obtained were ruled out of the study sample. These were mostly infants for whom adoption placement was planned, and who were not really in the limbo of temporary foster care. Also, the projected figures for adoption, based on the worker's initial plan, were small anyway, only 26 children, or 6% of the sample. In a sense, the adoption-plan cases in the sample represented relatively hard-to-place children, because a number of them had already been in foster care up to 3 years and none had been legally surrendered at the time of their entry into the study sample. It is noteworthy that these obstacles were overcome during the life of the project in only one of the 26 cases where adoption was planned.

Another alternative plan we had anticipated at the start of the study was specialized placement outside of the agency's foster care system. We had in mind placements in special facilities for the emotionally disturbed, the mentally retarded, the physically handicapped, etc. A total of six children, less than 2% of the sample, had been projected for specialized placement. Thus, this alternative plan was not viewed as a numerically important one from the beginning. As it turned out, three children were placed in residential treatment for emotional disturbance. All three were boys who had been in foster care placement in the Children's Center before they were transferred to the residential treatment facilities.

A third alternative plan was return to relatives other than parents. This plan, projected for only one child out of the 413 in the sample, was implemented for five children. Actually, six children were placed with with relatives, and this figure was reported in our preliminary findings,[17] but one was discharged during the first month (March 1971) and was not counted in the final study sample.

The placement of these children with their relatives appeared to be more planful than many of the returns to parents, since none of them had to be returned to foster care during the life of the project. This planfulness is attributable to the casework time and effort that had to go into the process of ruling out the possibility of return to parents and sometimes to getting the parent's agreement to place the child with relatives. Of the five children placed with relatives, four were boys; four were in foster family homes and one in the Children's Center prior to discharge; and they ranged in age from under 1 year to 8 years at time of admission to foster care. One had been in foster care less than 3 months, one between 6 months and a year, and the other three, over 2 years. The original reasons for their placement in foster care--physical neglect (2), emotional neglect (1), parent/child conflict (1), and parental unwillingness to care for the child (1)--suggest why discharge to relatives rather than return to parents was the plan implemented.

The alternative plan that accounted for the largest number of children who left temporary care was permanent foster care. As indicated earlier, this plan took on considerable importance as an option as we learned more about the constraints on the possibilities of return to parents or adoption in the study sample. That only 16 children, or 4% of the total sample, had permanent foster care plans implemented when the workers' projection was for 113 children, or 27% of the sample, to be in permanent foster care calls for some examination.

---

17. Shyne, et al., op. cit., p. 572.

At first there was some misunderstanding of and some objection on the part of the casework and supervisory staff to the term "permanent" foster care. In retrospect, it might have been better to use the expression "long-term" foster care, since the essential feature was that the child was almost certain to remain in foster care until his majority and foster care plans would be made in terms of that likelihood.

After the misunderstandings and objections were cleared up, there was an acceptance at least among the caseworkers that for considerable numbers of children in their caseloads "permanent" foster care was the only feasible alternative to the limbo of temporary foster care. However, when it came to implementing the plan the workers found it much more difficult than simply labeling a case as permanent foster care. The operational definition for implementation of the plan was that there be a clear understanding with parents and foster caretakers, documented in the agency record, that the child would probably remain in his current foster placement until he would reach majority age. Consequently, the only cases accepted as bona fide implemented permanent foster care plans were those in which there was documentation of understandings, with dates of those understandings, between agency workers, natural parents and foster parents that this plan seemed the most feasible (although not a binding) plan for the child.

In many cases workers felt that this was the de facto plan as far as all parties (workers, parents, caretakers and child) were concerned, but dates and documentation in the case records simply had not been established. Given the clerical backlog in dictation in the agency, it is clear that some cases that met all other criteria for permanent foster care did not meet the documentation criterion.

In other cases, although the workers thought that there was a de facto recognition by all parties in the foster care situation that permanent foster care was the only feasible plan, they were reluctant to make this recognition explicit and to formalize it. This reluctance was explained largely in terms of the anxiety formalization would provoke, particularly in the natural parents, who would have difficulty dealing with their guilt in having to admit that they could not in all likelihood have their child return to them during his childhood. If there was not an inability to admit this to themselves, there might be an inability to admit it to the child, which could be a contingency in a formal or explicit permanent foster care plan. In a number of cases it was as though a tenuous balance or equilibrium had been established in the foster care subsystem (child, parents, foster parents and worker) based on an implicit understanding of permanency and an explicit avowal or myth of imminent or near-imminent return of the child to his natural parents. While recognizing the lack of candor in such situations, the workers sometimes felt it was best not to threaten the equilibrium that had been established and not to risk a possible impulsive move, on the part of the natural parents, to take the child home even though they would be unable to maintain the child at home. This is not unlike the "neurotic arrangements" worked out in many intact families and marriages. That it should obtain in foster care situations should not be surprising. At the same time, it must be recognized that it leaves the child in a tenuous position.

Finally, the implementation of a permanent foster care plan was not possible, at least for some time, because one or more of the parties in the foster care subsystem would not accept the conditions required to implement it. For example, the foster caretaker might be willing to retain a child for a while, but not permanently. If return home, adoption or some other alternative were not available, it would be necessary to move the child to another foster care setting willing to keep him permanently. This, of course, would take time to prepare for and to bring about. Another possibility is that the child or parent could be adamantly against permanent foster care, despite all indications that nothing else would be possible.

Despite some of these difficulties and the casework time and effort required, 16 children had permanent foster care plans implemented during the project. These children differed somewhat from the children who had other permanent plans implemented, and their circumstances also were different. All 16 of the children were in foster family care rather than the Children's Center. Seven of them were boys and nine were girls. Their ages at admission to current foster care were rather evenly distributed across the range of under 1 year to 13 years. The modal age interval was 7 to 9 years, with four children in it. Eleven of the children were white, and five were nonwhite (four were black). As might have been expected, these children as a group had spent more time in their current foster homes than children in other disposition categories. The modal category of length of current stay in foster care for this group was from $1\frac{1}{2}$ to 2 years.

The most important reasons for their admission to foster care were: parents' emotional problem or mental illness (7), physical neglect (4), parental unwillingness to care for child (3), parent/child conflict (1), and child abuse (1). Perhaps more than any other circumstances, what differentiated the permanent foster care children from the others was that half of them had no mothers in their parental households. This was true for only 18% of the other children in the study sample. Whatever the reason for the mother's absence from the households--death, disappearance, etc.--the point is that there were fewer mothers to go home to for the permanent foster care children than for the others.

CHAPTER 5

DISCUSSION OF THE FINDINGS

It is advisable before discussing the findings to consider the research limitations
of the study. The methodological limitations were discussed to some extent in
Chapter 2. The aim here is to make sure the findings are seen within the context
of these limitations as we recapitulate their highlights.

Consideration of Research Limitations

It should be clear that the design of the research was not truly experimental.
Cases were not randomly assigned to the three segments of the study, as would
have been done in a more rigorous field experiment. Consequently, the words
"experimental" and "control" have been rather loosely used when applied to the
study segments.

The study illustrates some of the vagaries of trying to develop a quasi-
experimental design within the context of usual intake and practice in the agency
setting. Rather than using random assignment of cases to experimental and control groups, we opted for division of the existing caseload into three segments
of about equal size, into which approximately equal numbers of generally similar
cases were expected to be admitted. The unanticipated outcome, however, was
disproportionate numbers of new placements in the control and monitoring segments.
This left the special worker segment at somewhat of a disadvantage on the important
variable of length of time the child was in foster care.

However, we do not say in retrospect that we should have insisted upon random assignment of cases to segments, or barred transfer of cases among segments during the life of the project. We were able to take into account by statistical means some of the effect of the bias in the time variable and in other variables.

There is some question whether the additional rigor of random assignment and other experimental procedures would have been worth the disruption and procedural constraints on agency practice. Would enough have been gained in permitting valid conclusions, given the lack of as many cases or as much time as desirable to test the effectiveness of the strategies? Questions of this type are perennial for researchers in the general area of human services, and perhaps the answers are unique to the circumstances and the researchers.

We did not see the research as simply a test of the particular strategies involved. We knew from prior research that variables other than the "experimental" ones could have a profound effect on the discharge or retention of children in foster care. An attempt was made to take these variables into account, to collect data on them systematically, and thus to set the stage for learning more about the total situation than just the effect of the intervention strategies. It was this broader perspective for gaining knowledge that led us to undertake the research with a smaller sample and less time than we would have liked.

Another question of strategy is raised by this research. Should a demonstration be undertaken in an agency setting that by intention, and even to some extent by design, has already tried to do something about the problem being researched? The setting for the study reported in "An Agency Cleans House," cited earlier, was an agency that was admittedly backward in dealing with the problem of children adrift in foster care (as documented by Maas and Engler), and that had a lot of catching up to do in its practice.[1] Since it had much to gain and little to

lose, it was able to show dramatic changes in the numbers of children taken out

of the limbo of foster care within 1½ or 2 years.

In contrast, the agency involved in this study was strongly committed to the

prevention of placement and to reestablishing the child with his family whenever

possible. The agency had even used a monitoring form of sorts, though it was not

so systematically applied as in this study. The question, then, can be raised:

Why pick a setting that did not have much room for improvement? Perhaps the only

answer is another question: Why not pick an agency that wants to improve its

practice even more? That the agency is motivated and willing to take on the

added burdens of demonstration and evaluation provides the answer.

Highlights of the Findings

Given the methodological limitations, it is not possible to say definitively

that the intervention strategies did or did not "work." It can perhaps be said

that, within the limitations of time and numbers, it could not be demonstrated

to a statistically significant degree that the intervention strategies worked

better than regular practice. Indeed, there is some evidence for the rather

ironic conclusion that planful attempts to work with and prepare natural parents

for return of their children from foster care (as was done by the special workers

in this project) is more time-consuming and less likely to show rapid discharge

rates than regular practice. It appears that in the normal course of events in

practice the parent is likely to take the initiative in bringing about the return

of the child. Some of these returns might be precipitous and ill-advised in

terms of the parents' circumstances or financial or emotional ability at the

time, but if the placement was voluntary to begin with (as most were in this

study) the parent could demand and get the child returned. It is probably in

those cases in which workers have not been in contact or working planfully with

_____

1. Paull, op. cit.

the parent that precipitous returns come about. Apparently a price is paid for this, as evidenced by the fact that 20 of 72, or 28%, of the children discharged to parents or other relatives in cases not handled by the special workers were returned to foster care before the project ended, whereas none of the nine children whose discharges were arranged by the special workers were returned.

On the basis of prior research in foster care, there was reason to think that certain antecedent or baseline variables would show a stronger statistical relationship to retention or discharge of children from foster care than the intervention variables. This turned out to be the case, beginning with the central variable of time spent by the child in his current foster care placement. As already mentioned, the distribution of this variable within the study segments was uneven, with the special worker segment containing significantly more children who had been in care more than a year. This had to be taken into account (controlled for) in assessing the impact of the intervention strategies, but the direct relationship between time in care and frequency of discharge to parents was very strong and statistically significant ($p < .001$). As had been shown by Maas and Engler, and by several others since, the longer the child remains in foster care, the poorer are his chances of returning home. The intervention strategies were unable to overcome this strong relationship in a statistical sense within the limitations of sample size.

In reviewing the factors that were found to be significantly associated with the implementation of definite plans for the children, particularly return to their parents, it became evident that many of the factors that distinguish placement decisions from decisions to serve children in their own homes were operating. As had been found in the Child Welfare League's study, Factors Associated With Placement Decisions, severe problems in the mother's behavior, her physical and emotional care of the child, and her supervision and guidance of the child before placement were associated with placement (in this instance, retention in placement) and less severe problems with service in own home (in this study, discharges to parents).[2]

On the other hand, the children's behavior and emotional adjustment did not show the same relationship to the placement/own-home dichotomy as in the Factors study, where acting-out, antisocial behaviors were found to be more frequent in placement situations. That did not show up in this study in retention in placement versus discharge, but children's problems as the primary reason for placement in the first place simply did not apply to many cases. However, items such as the child's emotional attachment to his natural mother or to his foster mother were significantly related to outcome. The stronger the attachment to the natural mother, the more likely was return home, and the stronger the attachment to the foster mother, the more likely was retention in foster care.

A variable that probably reflects the mother's attachment to the child and her desire for him to return home is her frequency of contacts with the child in foster care. This variable showed a strong, statistically significant relationship ($p < .001$) to the child's return to the parental home. This is of course an expected finding, and one that has some implications for practice.

The importance of environmental factors came through repeatedly in the findings. The adequacy of the parents' housing was found to be significantly related to the return of the children to their parents. The more adequate the housing, the more likely was discharge of the child to the home. As to family financial conditions, significantly more children were returned to parents who were receiving full or supplementary public assistance than to those who were not. This

_____

2. Phillips, et al., op. cit.

speaks to the dire economic circumstances of the families not receiving assistance, rather than to the "adequacy" of the public assistance grants.

Environmental factors also entered strongly into the issue of whether or not children had to be returned to foster care. Data from followup interviews with the families after discharge showed that significantly more children from families with inadequate housing and income had to be returned to foster care. The interview data on emotional adjustment or pathology in the parents did not show the same relationship to return to foster care as did the environmental factors.

Finally, it was found that the discharged children who did not have to be returned to foster care showed positive change in their general well-being from the time of the first followup interview to the second interview 4 months later.

Implications for Practice

It is perhaps a truism to say that field research has an effect on the events and practices it sets out to study. It would be expected that a field demonstration such as this would have an effect, because that is what it is intended to do. However, even before introduction of the intervention strategies, the process of setting up systematic procedures for data collection and case selection in this study effected an attitudinal if not substantive change in the appraisal of the study problem by the practitioners who had been dealing with it in their everyday work.

This showed up first in the projected plan for each child in the foster care sample, as indicated by the caseworkers on the Baseline Data Form. The initial expectation, particularly among the agency's administrative and supervisory staff, was that the plan for most of the children in foster care would be for return to their families. This was in line with the general philosophy and intent of the agency program. It was thought that there would be practically no children for whom permanent or long-term foster care would be the projected plan. Yet, the workers' projected plans on the Baseline Forms showed that only 32% of the children were expected to return to their parents and fully 27% of the children were expected to require permanent foster care. This recalls the Girls at Vocational High study in which the administrators of Youth Consultation Service were convinced that their services to the experimental group of girls would bring about significantly greater gains than would occur among the control group girls.[3] The social workers who were supposed to provide those services, however, were much less optimistic about effecting such gains. Perhaps this finding has more implication for research than for practice, namely that researchers should be sure to get the views of line service staff before hypothesizing differences between experimental and control groups.

There was a similar finding of undue optimism among the workers in the control segment of this study concerning the number of children projected for return to parents, as compared with the workers in the two experimental segments, who had to fill out periodic monitoring forms and to account for their activities and progress toward the projected plans. A significant effect of the monitoring intervention strategy was that its accountability features made the workers more realistic in their appraisals and plans for the foster children. The implication for practice is that administrative and caseload planning would be better served by using such an accountability mechanism rather than a simple, "one-shot" projection by the workers. Although the workers may choose the less optimistic alternatives more frequently under such a setup, this does not rule out their doing something about the problem. The fact that the special workers had greater relative success in implementing the permanent foster care plan

3. Henry Meyer et al., Girls at Vocational High: An Experiment in Social Work Intervention (New York: Russell Sage Foundation, 1965).

illustrates this point. This was probably because they were under more direct pressure to demonstrate some kind of result or definite plan in their work with the natural parents than were the other workers. The implication is that the monitoring-accountability system should be backed by some kind of pressure; concerned, periodic (but not routinized) supervisory review might provide this.

What are the practice implications for the use of special workers to work intensively with natural parents, based on the findings of this study? The special worker segment did not show significantly more implemented plans than the other two study segments. The two special workers themselves directly served 37 children in 24 families, and of these seven children were returned to their parents, two were returned to other relatives, and five had permanent foster care plans formalized and implemented. It was found that considerably more planfulness and service contact were involved in the implementation of definite plans and in postdischarge service by the special workers, and this was probably the reason none of the nine children discharged to their parents or other relatives by the special workers had to be returned to foster care during the study. This contrasted with a 28% rate of return to foster care of children in cases handled by other workers.

It may be noted that, if two children were kept out of foster care in the Children's Center of the study agency for a year, the saving in cost would pay the salary of one special worker. But who can say that more effort on the part of regular agency workers to work with the natural parents could not achieve such stable discharges? If the effort were made, and if things did not drift back to foster care "business as usual" with the natural parents as outsiders, there is no reason why stable discharges could not be achieved.

Apropos of this, the finding that significantly more returns home occurred for children who were more frequently visited by their mothers in foster care underscores the observation by a natural parent that workers would do well, except in certain cases, to push natural parents into visiting their children early and regularly after placement in foster care.[4]

Finally, the findings from followup interviews with families of children discharged from foster care indicate that the well-being of the children is enhanced by the return and that followup services after discharge are crucial to prevent return of the child to foster care. The services that seem most needed are help with problems of income and housing, and the sustaining emotional support and interest of workers responsible for the case. To deny these aftercare services in many instances would risk unnecessary return of the child to foster care and perhaps the start of the all-too-common and destructive cycle of entry, exit and reentry into foster care.

---

4. McAdams, op. cit.

CWIA Return Home Project

Form C

MONITORING FORM -- Quarterly Report

Name of child _____ Case No. _____ Worker _____

1. Worker's present plan for child: Return to parent home ___ Permanent foster care ___
   Adoption ___ Other (specify) _____

2. Has the plan been carried out? Yes _____* Date _____
                                  No _____   Date likely to be carried out
                                              (month & year) _____

3. If plan has not been carried out, please indicate below: a) main factors interfering
   with plan, b) worker activities in past 3 months to accomplish plan, c) activities
   planned for next 3 months toward this end.

	a) Interfering factors	b) Worker activities past 3 months	c) Worker activities next 3 months
Re child			
Re parents			
Re external situation			

*Plan for "permanent foster care" is considered as carried out when there is a clear
understanding with parents and foster caretakers, documented in the record, that child's
present placement is permanent.

Plan for "adoption" is considered as carried out when child is placed in an adoptive
home and parental rights have been terminated.

Reviewed by Supervisor: Name _____ Date _____

CWLA Return Home Project
February 1971 -- Form B

```
┌──────────────┐
│              │
└──────────────┘
```

BASELINE DATA ON STUDY CHILD

Name of Child_____ Case No._____ Worker_____

Sex (circle letter) M F Birthdate_____ Birthplace_____

Race (circle number) 1 White 2 Negro 3 Other, specify_____

I. Child's Current Admission to Foster Care (that is, last separation from natural or adoptive family)

1. Date of child's current admission to foster care_____

2. Were any other children from this family admitted to foster care at the same time?

        Yes ____ How many?_____
        No ____

3. Were any other children already in foster care?

        Yes ____ How many?_____
        No ____

4. Check the single most important reason for the child's current admission to foster care.

    ____Child's physical handicap or disability
    ____Child's mental retardation
    ____Child's emotional or behavior problem

    ____Abuse of child
    ____Physical neglect of child
    ____Emotional neglect of child

    ____Parent-child conflict
    ____Marital conflict
    ____Antisocial behavior of parent(s)

    ____Physical illness or disability of parent(s)
    ____Emotional problem or mental illness of parent(s)
    ____Employment of caretaking parent

    ____Death of caretaking parent
    ____Parent unwilling to take care of child
    ____Financial need
    ____Inadequate housing

Child's Name: First_____ Last_____

5. Household from which child was last admitted to foster care

   A. Adults in household (check all that apply)

        _____Mother
        _____Father
        _____"Stepmother" (legal or non-legal)
        _____"Stepfather" (legal or non-legal)
        _____Other adult relatives
        _____Nonrelated adults

   B. Other children in household (give number in each category)

        _____Older siblings
        _____Younger siblings
        _____Other children

   C. Whereabouts of mother and/or father if not in household. (Be sure to answer for both mother and father if both are out of household.)

Mother		Father
_____	Deceased............................	_____
_____	Hospital or other institution........	_____
_____	Living with another "marital" partner	_____
_____	Elsewhere (specify).................	_____
_____	Unknown.............................	_____

                If absence from household was
                regarded as temporary, how long was
_____   the absence anticipated to last?   _____

II. The Child at Time of Current Admission to Foster Care

   1. Approximately how long had child lived previously in each of the following settings? (Note that the total of the items should equal the child's age.)

Yrs. Mos.
____ ____ Home of one or both natural parents
____ ____ Home of relatives
____ ____ Foster family home
____ ____ Group home or institution for dependent children
____ ____ Residential treatment or psychiatric institution
____ ____ Institution for mentally retarded
____ ____ Correctional institution
____ ____ Elsewhere (specify)_____

   2. Had child entered school?

        Yes____ Specify last grade completed_____
        No ____

Child's Name: First_____ Last_____

3. Circle number to indicate child's estimated intellectual level.

      1 Above average
      2 Average
      3 Somewhat below average
      4 Well below average
      5 Unknown

4. Problems in the child's behavior and adjustment at the time of current admission to foster care.

For each of the items below, enter a check in the column that best describes the child's functioning.

Area of Functioning	No Problem	Moderate Problem	Severe Problem	Unknown	Not Applicable
A. Family functioning 1. Relations with parents (such as hostile, fearful, rejects control, overly dependent)					
2. Relations with siblings					
B. School functioning 1. Learning problems					
2. Behavior problems (including truancy as well as classroom behavior)					
C. Physical functioning 1. Physical disability					
2. Frequent or chronic illness					
D. Behavior and emotional adjustment (such as withdrawn, eating difficulties, uncontrollable temper, stealing, fighting, sexual acting out)					
E. Social functioning in community 1. In relation to peers (such as lack of friends of own age group, associating with anti-social peer group)					
2. In relation to adults (such as provocative behavior with neighbors, police, store-keepers)					

Child's Name: First_____ Last_____

5. If any problems in the child's behavior and adjustment were significant factors in his admission to foster care, please describe briefly the nature of the problem.

_____

_____

_____

_____

_____

_____

III. The Child's Parents -- Please reply in terms of the natural or adoptive parents. If only one parent is living, record data for that parent only.

<table>
<tr><td>Mother</td><td>Father</td></tr>
</table>

1. Status of parent (circle)

Mother	Father
1 Natural parent	1 Natural parent
2 Adoptive parent	2 Adoptive parent
3 Deceased (skip to Section IV)	3 Deceased (skip to Section IV)

2. Age at Child's Current Admission to Foster Care

_____   _____

3. Race (circle)

Mother	Father
1 White	1 White
2 Negro	2 Negro
3 Other (specify)_____	3 Other (specify)_____

4. Religion (circle)

Mother	Father
1 Protestant	1 Protestant
2 Catholic	2 Catholic
3 Jewish	3 Jewish
4 Other	4 Other
5 Unknown	5 Unknown

5. Last school grade completed

_____   _____

Child's Name: First_____ Last_____

Mother   Father

6. Estimated intellectual level (circle)

Mother	Father
1 Above average	1 Above average
2 Average	2 Average
3 Somewhat below average	3 Somewhat below average
4 Well below average	4 Well below average
5 Unknown	5 Unknown

7. Usual occupation

_____   _____

Please answer questions 8-20 in terms of the parents' situation and functioning at the time of the child's current admission to foster care. (Circle appropriate number.)

Mother   Father

8. Work Status

Mother	Father
1 Employed full-time	1 Employed full-time
2 Employed part-time	2 Employed part-time
3 Unemployed, seeking work	3 Unemployed, seeking work
4 Not employed nor seeking work	4 Not employed nor seeking work
5 Unknown	5 Unknown

9. Physical illness or disability that interferes with functioning

Mother	Father
1 None	1 None
2 Yes, not hospitalized	2 Yes, not hospitalized
3 Yes, hospitalized	3 Yes, hospitalized
4 Unknown	4 Unknown

10. Mental illness that seriously interferes with functioning

Mother	Father
1 None	1 None
2 Yes, not hospitalized	2 Yes, not hospitalized
3 Yes, hospitalized	3 Yes, hospitalized
4 Unknown	4 Unknown

11. Marital functioning (continuity, affection, supportiveness in current "marital" relationship)

Mother	Father
1 No problem	1 No problem
2 Moderate problem	2 Moderate problem
3 Severe problem	3 Severe problem
4 Unknown	4 Unknown
5 Not applicable (no spouse)	5 Not applicable (no spouse)

Child's Name: First_____   Last_____

Mother   Father

12. Household management and housekeeping
    practices (cleanliness, maintenance,
    food provision, etc.)

1 No problem	1 No problem
2 Moderate problem	2 Moderate problem
3 Severe problem	3 Severe problem
4 Unknown	4 Unknown

13. Financial management
    (budgeting and use of money)

1 No problem	1 No problem
2 Moderate problem	2 Moderate problem
3 Severe problem	3 Severe problem
4 Unknown	4 Unknown

14. Employment functioning (job stability,
    work performance, relations with co-
    workers and superiors)

1 No problem	1 No problem
2 Moderate problem	2 Moderate problem
3 Severe problem	3 Severe problem
4 Unknown	4 Unknown
5 Not applicable (not in labor market)	5 Not applicable (not in labor market)

15. Social functioning in community (isolation
    from or involvement with neighbors, com-
    munity groups and activities)

1 No problem	1 No problem
2 Moderate problem	2 Moderate problem
3 Severe problem	3 Severe problem
4 Unknown	4 Unknown

16. Behavior and emotional adjustment

   a. Behavior (such as excessive drinking,
      use of drugs, sexual promiscuity, etc.)

1 No problem	1 No problem
2 Moderate problem	2 Moderate problem
3 Severe problem	3 Severe problem
4 Unknown	4 Unknown

Child's Name: First_____ Last_____

<u>Mother</u>   <u>Father</u>

　　　　b. Emotional adjustment (such as
　　　　　　depressed, withdrawn, suspicious)

1　No problem   1　No problem
2　Moderate problem   2　Moderate problem
3　Severe problem   3　Severe problem
4　Unknown   4　Unknown

　　　17. <u>Physical care of child</u> (such as
　　　　　 inattention to feeding, clothing,
　　　　　 hygiene, medical needs, protection
　　　　　 from physical danger)

1　No problem   1　No problem
2　Moderate problem   2　Moderate problem
3　Severe problem   3　Severe problem
4　Unknown   4　Unknown

　　　18. <u>Emotional care of child</u> (such as lack
　　　　　 of warmth, affection, concern)

1　No problem   1　No problem
2　Moderate problem   2　Moderate problem
3　Severe problem   3　Severe problem
4　Unknown   4　Unknown

　　　19. <u>Supervision, guidance and training of</u>
　　　　　 <u>child</u> (such as overly severe punishments,
　　　　　 erratic handling, laxness in discipline,
　　　　　 expectations too high, failure to set limits)

1　No problem   1　No problem
2　Moderate problem   2　Moderate problem
3　Severe problem   3　Severe problem
4　Unknown   4　Unknown

Child's Name: First_____ Last_____

20. If any problems in the behavior and adjustment of the parents were significant factors in the child's admission to foster care, please describe briefly the nature of the problem.

_____

_____

_____

_____

_____

_____

_____

_____

IV. External Circumstances at Time of Child's Current Admission to Foster Care

    1. Estimated total weekly income from all sources of household from which child was admitted to care:

        $_____

    2. Was family receiving public assistance?

        1 Yes -- full
        2 Yes -- supplementary
        3 No
        4 Unknown

    3. Housing

      a. Adequacy of space and facilities
        1 Adequate
        2 Marginal
        3 Inadequate
        4 Unknown

      b. Freedom from hazards to health and safety
        1 Adequate
        2 Marginal
        3 Inadequate
        4 Unknown

Child's Name: First_____ Last_____

4. Suitability of neighborhood

       1 Adequate
       2 Marginal
       3 Inadequate
       4 Unknown

5. Availability of relatives for moral support or practical help

       1 Available and helpful
       2 Available but helpfulness not known
       3 Available but not helpful
       4 No relatives available
       5 Unknown

6. Availability of friends, neighbors

       1 Available and helpful
       2 Available but helpfulness not known
       3 Available but not helpful
       4 Household socially isolated
       5 Unknown

7. If any problems in the external circumstances of the family (1-6 above) were significant factors in the child's admission to foster care, describe briefly the nature of the problem.

_____

_____

_____

_____

_____

_____

V. Potential for Child's Return Home at the Present Time -- Be sure to enter a check in each column that applies.

1. Parents' attitude toward child's return home   Mother   Father

Eager for child's return...................................... _____ _____
Moderately interested in child's return................... _____ _____
Mixed feelings... _____ _____
Moderately opposed to return home......................... _____ _____
Strongly opposed to return home........................... _____ _____
Unknown... _____ _____

Child's Name: First _____ Last _____

2. If either parent is moderately or strongly opposed to   Mother   Father
   return home, what is his attitude toward surrender?

    Never discussed.. ____ ____
    Discussed, very resistant to surrender...................... ____ ____
    Discussed, moderately resistant............................. ____ ____
    Discussed, considering surrender............................ ____ ____
    Not known whether discussed................................. ____ ____
    Not applicable -- not opposed to return..................... ____ ____

3. Parents' contact with child over past few months

    At least once a week.. ____ ____
    About once in two weeks..................................... ____ ____
    About once a month.. ____ ____
    Some contact but less than once a month..................... ____ ____
    No contact.. ____ ____
    Not applicable -- child in care less than one month........ ____ ____

4. If child's mother or father is living with a partner
   other than the child's natural parent, what is the
   attitude of that partner to the child's return to his   Mother's Father's
   or her household?   Partner Partner

    Eager for child's return................................... ____ ____
    Moderately interested in child's return.................... ____ ____
    Mixed feelings... ____ ____
    Moderately opposed to return home.......................... ____ ____
    Strongly opposed to return home............................ ____ ____
    Unknown.. ____ ____
    Not applicable... ____ ____

5. Child's attitude toward return   Child

    Eager to return home right away............................ ____
    Moderately interested in returning home.................... ____
    Mixed feelings... ____
    Somewhat reluctant to return home.......................... ____
    Very reluctant to return home.............................. ____
    Too young to express a preference.......................... ____
    Unknown.. ____

6. Child's expectation of length of stay in foster care

    Expects to return home soon................................ ____
    Expects to return home but not in immediate future......... ____
    Expects to remain in foster care indefinitely.............. ____
    Too young to have clear expectation........................ ____
    Unknown.. ____

Child's Name: First_____ Last_____

7. Child's attachment to his
parents and his foster parents (or
persons principally responsible for   Foster   Foster
his care in institution)   Mother   Father   Mother   Father

    Very strong emotional tie.............. _____   _____   _____   _____
    Moderately strong..................... _____   _____   _____   _____
    Slightly weak......................... _____   _____   _____   _____
    Very weak............................. _____   _____   _____   _____
    No emotional tie...................... _____   _____   _____   _____
    Unknown............................... _____   _____   _____   _____

                                                                              Foster   Foster

8. Foster parents' interest in child's remaining with them   Mother   Father

    Would like to adopt child.................................... _____   _____
    Would like child to remain permanently without adoption.. _____   _____
    Glad to have child remain as long as necessary but not
    permanently.. _____   _____
    Reluctant to have child remain any longer................ _____   _____
    Insistent on other arrangements for child as early as
    possible.. _____   _____
    Not applicable -- child in institution................... _____   _____
    Unknown... _____   _____

9. Worker's plan for child   Worker

    No plan as yet.. _____
    Return to parent(s)' home................................... _____
    Permanent foster care....................................... _____
    Adoption.. _____

    Other (specify)_____

10. Worker's degree of certainty about being able to carry out
plan   Worker

    High.. _____
    Moderate.. _____
    Low... _____
    Not applicable -- no plan as yet........................ _____

11. Worker's judgment of how much longer child will continue
in care away from home

    Less than three months..................................... _____
    Three months but under six months.......................... _____
    Six months but under one year.............................. _____
    One year but under three years............................. _____
    Three years but not permanently............................ _____
    Permanently... _____

Child's Name: First_____ Last_____

12. Child's Total Well-Being: To what extent does this child have the physical, intellectual, emotional and social abilities and resources to weather his life situations?

      Extremely high total well-being. This child will be able to handle anything. He'll make out fine regardless of the situation.. _____

      Markedly high total well-being. This child will have difficulties only under situations of extreme pressure. He will weather with ease anything he's likely to meet...... _____

      Slightly above average well-being. This child will handle anything that the average child will, but perhaps with more ease than most... _____

      About average well-being. This child will handle adequately the kind of life situations he is likely to meet. A situation of unusual stress might be beyond his abilities, however... _____

      Slightly below average well-being. This child will handle anything that the average child will, but perhaps with more difficulty than most.. _____

      Markedly low total well-being. This child will handle his life situations adequately only if he is in a supporting environment. In ordinary life situations, some protection should be available for the times he will need it.......... _____

      Extremely low total well-being. This child will have difficulty in successfully weathering anything but the simplest type of situation. He will need constant protection in even ordinary life situations................ _____

Date Form Completed_____

CWLA Return Home Project

EVALUATION INTERVIEW I

Form G

Child Welfare League of America

March 1971

◇

EVALUATION INTERVIEW I

Name of Child (first) _____ (last) _____ Date Discharged _____

Name of Respondent(s) _____

Address _____

Telephone _____ Date of Interview _____

I. Household Information

1. Adults currently living in household (check all that apply)

    Mother
    Father   _____
    "Stepmother" (legal or nonlegal)   _____
    "Stepfather" (legal or nonlegal)   _____
    Other adult relatives   _____
    Non-related adults   _____

2. Other children in household (give number of each)

    Older siblings
    Younger siblings   _____
    Other children   _____

3. Are any members of the family currently absent from the household?

    Yes_____   No_____

    If yes, a) Who (relationship to child) _____

             b) Where (e.g. hospital, relatives)_____

             c) Anticipated length of absence _____

4. What members of the household were: Interviewed? Seen? (Check all that apply)
                    Interviewed   Seen
    Mother
    Father   _____   _____
    "Stepmother"   _____   _____
    "Stepfather"   _____   _____
    Child   _____   _____
    Sibling(s)   _____   _____
    Other (specify)   _____   _____   _____

Child's Name: First _____ Last _____

5. Was the child interviewed separately at any time during the contact?

   Yes_____ No_____

II. Child's Current Functioning

Areas of Functioning:

	Parent Statement	Child Statement	Interviewer Evaluation
1. Relations with parents			
No problem	_____	_____	_____
Moderate problem	_____	_____	_____
Severe problem	_____	_____	_____
Unknown	_____	_____	_____
Not applicable	_____	_____	_____
2. Relations with siblings			
No problem	_____	_____	_____
Moderate problem	_____	_____	_____
Severe problem	_____	_____	_____
Unknown	_____	_____	_____
Not applicable	_____	_____	_____

3. Is child entered in school? Yes_____ ; Grade _____
   No_____ ; Skip to #6.

	Parent Statement	Child Statement	Interviewer Evaluation
4. Learning problems			
No problem	_____	_____	_____
Moderate problem	_____	_____	_____
Severe problem	_____	_____	_____
Unknown	_____	_____	_____
5. School behavior			
No problem	_____	_____	_____
Moderate problem	_____	_____	_____
Severe problem	_____	_____	_____
Unknown	_____	_____	_____
6. Physical disability			
No problem	_____	_____	_____
Moderate problem	_____	_____	_____
Severe problem	_____	_____	_____
Unknown	_____	_____	_____

Child's Name: First _____ Last _____

	Parent Statement	Child Statement	Interviewer Evaluation
7. Frequent or chronic illness			
No problem	_____	_____	_____
Moderate problem	_____	_____	_____
Severe problem	_____	_____	_____
Unknown	_____	_____	_____
8. Behavior and emotional adjustment			
No problem	_____	_____	_____
Moderate problem	_____	_____	_____
Severe problem	_____	_____	_____
Unknown	_____	_____	_____
9. Peer relations			
No problem	_____	_____	_____
Moderate problem	_____	_____	_____
Severe problem	_____	_____	_____
Unknown	_____	_____	_____
10. Relations with adults (other than parents)			
No problem	_____	_____	_____
Moderate problem	_____	_____	_____
Severe problem	_____	_____	_____
Unknown	_____	_____	_____

11. If you think there are any problems in the child's adjustment or behavior that might interfere with his remaining at home, briefly describe the nature of the problems.

_____

_____

_____

_____

_____

_____

_____

_____

-4-

Child's Name: First _____ Last _____

III. Parent(s)' Current Functioning

Areas of Functioning:

Interviewer Evaluation

	Mother	Father
1. Relations with child since discharge		
No problem	_____	_____
Moderate problem	_____	_____
Severe problem	_____	_____
Unknown	_____	_____
2. Marital functioning		
No problem	_____	_____
Moderate problem	_____	_____
Severe problem	_____	_____
Unknown	_____	_____
Not applicable (no spouse)	_____	_____
3. Work status		
Employed full-time	_____	_____
Employed part-time	_____	_____
Unemployed, seeking work	_____	_____
Not employed or seeking work	_____	_____
Unknown	_____	_____
4. Financial management		
No problem	_____	_____
Moderate problem	_____	_____
Severe problem	_____	_____
Unknown	_____	_____
5. Household management and housekeeping practices		
No problem	_____	_____
Moderate problem	_____	_____
Severe problem	_____	_____
Unknown	_____	_____
6. Physical functioning (illness or disability)		
No problem	_____	_____
Moderate problem	_____	_____
Severe problem	_____	_____
Unknown	_____	_____

Child's Name: First _____ Last _____

	Interviewer Evaluation	
	Mother	Father

7. Behavior problems

      No problem
      Moderate problem
      Severe problem
      Unknown

8. Emotional adjustment

      No problem
      Moderate problem
      Severe problem
      Unknown

9. Social functioning in community

      No problem
      Moderate problem
      Severe problem
      Unknown

10. Physical care of child

      No problem
      Moderate problem
      Severe problem
      Unknown

11. Emotional care of child

      No problem
      Moderate problem
      Severe problem
      Unknown

12. Supervision, guidance and
     training of child

      No problem
      Moderate problem
      Severe problem
      Unknown

Child's Name: First _____ Last _____

13. Family cohesion as noted by interviewer

    Exceptionally close, warm family relations
    Closely knit, cooperative   _____
    Fair cohesiveness with minor problems   _____
    Considerable tension or lack of warmth   _____
    Severe conflict or absence of affectional ties   _____
    Unknown - insufficient observational or interview data   _____

14. If you think there are any problems in parental or family functioning that might interfere with the child's remaining at home, briefly describe the problems.

_____

_____

_____

_____

_____

_____

IV. Current External Circumstances of the Family

1. Adequacy of household income

    More than adequate
    Adequate   _____
    Inadequate   _____
    Grossly inadequate   _____
    Insufficient data to judge   _____

2. Is family currently receiving public assistance?

    Yes - full
    Yes - supplementary   _____
    No   _____

3. Adequacy of housing in space and facilities

    Adequate
    Marginal   _____
    Inadequate   _____

4. Freedom of housing from hazards to health and safety

    Adequate
    Marginal   _____
    Inadequate   _____

Child's Name: First _____ Last _____

5. Suitability of neighborhood (for raising children)

      Adequate   _____

      Marginal   _____

      Inadequate   _____

6. Availability of relatives for moral support or practical help

      Available and helpful   _____

      Available but helpfulness

           not known   _____

      Available but not helpful _____

      No relatives available

7. Availability of friends or neighbors

      Available and helpful   _____

      Available but helpfulness

           not known   _____

      Available but not helpful _____

      Household socially isolated _____

8. If you think there are any problems in the external circumstances of the family that might interfere with the child's remaining at home, briefly describe the problems.

_____

_____

_____

_____

_____

_____

V. _Prognostic Information_   Interviewer Evaluation

	Mother	Father
1. Parents' attitude toward child's return home (at point of return)		
Eager for return	_____	_____
Moderately interested in return	_____	_____
Mixed feelings	_____	_____
Moderately opposed to return	_____	_____
Strongly opposed to return	_____	_____
Unknown	_____	_____

Child's Name: First _____ Last _____

	Interviewer Evaluation	
	Mother	Father

2. Child's attachment to his parents

      Very strong emotional tie   _____   _____
      Moderately strong   _____   _____
      Slightly weak   _____   _____
      Very weak   _____   _____
      No emotional tie   _____   _____
      Unknown   _____   _____

3. Child's attitude toward return (at point of return)

      Eager to return   _____
      Interested in returning   _____
      Mixed feelings   _____
      Somewhat reluctant to return   _____
      Very reluctant to return   _____
      Too young to express a preference   _____
      Unknown   _____

4. Child's Total Well-Being: To what extent does this child have the physical, intellectual, emotional and social abilities and resources to weather his life situations?

Extremely high total well-being. This child will be able to handle anything. He'll make out fine regardless of the situation.   _____

Markedly high total well-being. This child will have difficulties only under situations of extreme pressure. He will weather with ease anything he's likely to meet.   _____

Slightly above average well-being. This child will handle anything that the average child will, but perhaps with more ease than most.   _____

About average well-being. This child will handle adequately the kind of life situations he is likely to meet. A situation of unusual stress might be beyond his abilities, however.   _____

Slightly below average well-being. This child will handle anything that the average child will, but perhaps with more difficulty than most.   _____

Markedly low total well-being. This child will handle his life situations adequately only if he is in a supporting environment. In ordinary life situations, some protection should be available for the times he will need it.   _____

Extremely low total well-being. This child will have difficulty in successfully weathering anything but the simplest type of situation. He will need constant protection in even ordinary life situations.   _____

Child's Name: First _____ Last _____

5. Probability of child's being able to remain in parental home

Very good   _____
Good   _____
50 - 50   _____
Poor   _____
Very poor   _____

VI. Interviewer Comments

1. Respondent's (parent's) general attitude toward you

Very responsive, frank, open
Responsive but somewhat cautious   _____
Guarded, suspicious, minimal answers   _____
Very unresponsive, hostile   _____

2. Child's general attitude toward your questions

Very responsive, open
Responsive but cautious   _____
Guarded, fearful or suspicious   _____
Very unresponsive, very fearful or hostile   _____
Not applicable   _____

3. Respondent's willingness to be interviewed again in four months

Yes, definitely willing
Yes, probably   _____
Not sure   _____
Probably not   _____
Definitely not   _____

4. Degree of certainty you feel about your evaluations in general (Sections I - V)

Very certain
Fairly certain   _____
50 - 50   _____
Fairly uncertain   _____
Very uncertain   _____

Child's Name: First _____ Last _____

5. Comments: (Note any observations that might clarify or expand upon any of the foregoing information. Include also points of information that should be followed up in the next interview)

_____

_____

_____

_____

_____

_____

_____

_____

_____

_____

_____

_____

_____

_____

_____

_____

_____

_____

_____

_____

_____

_____

_____

_____

_____